Praise for
Pixels and Place

The age-old push and pull between form and function in design conversations usually misses a key question: function for whom? Now as the intermingling of online and physical worlds becomes a constant in modern life, it's time to address our ability to answer that question. The constant data trail streaming from individual experience can power ever-greater meaning, utility, and profit in daily life — if we can just drop the tech buzzwords and realize that through all of it, people just want to do things, feel something, connect, and remember. This is a topic that needs exploring right now and I can't think of a better explorer than Kate O'Neill.

— *Gavin Ivester, founding partner at FLO | Thinkery; former product, design, brand, and innovation leader at Gibson Guitar, Nike, and Apple*

We all straddle our "real" and "online" lives with various degrees of success. The rules are being made up as we go along, and it is very difficult to remain completely off the grid and still participate in modern life. Kate O'Neill explores what we are gaining and losing in this transition, and what it means to be human in the digital age.

— *Tim Ash, CEO of SiteTuners, Author of Landing Page Optimization, and Founder of Conversion Conference*

You might have kick-ass advertising, retail, customer service, data analysis, mobile development and digital teams. If you do, then congratulations! While they may all do a great job, your customers experience your brand differently. They expect their interaction with

you to be seamless and uniform. Their buyer journey skips around between pixels, devices, and places. Kate O'Neill's "Pixels and Place" is an important book that will introduce you to the concept of Human Experience Design. Buy this book, read it, share it with your colleagues and learn how to integrate data and empathy to build deeper relationships with your customers.
— *Jeffrey Eisenberg, author of NY Times Bestsellers "Waiting For Your Cat To Bark?" and "Call To Action"*

Kate O'Neill understands that the "Internet of Things" is first and foremost an Internet of people. Let her guide you toward your brand's greatest opportunity to stand out and succeed by designing intentionally for meaningful human experiences in the space where "online" and the real world converge.
— *Jeffrey Zeldman, author, Designing With Web Standards*

"Pixels and Places" addresses the emerging importance of elements that create human experiences worthy of remembering. To build empathy with users, a design-centric organization empowers employees to observe behavior and draw conclusions about what people want and need. Those conclusions are tremendously hard to express in quantitative language. Instead, organizations that "get" design use emotional language (words that concern desires, aspirations, engagement, and experience) to describe products and users. "Pixels and Places" lays out the roadmap for thinking to accomplish that aim. Needed by any organization that desires to succeed in the Digital Age.
— *Jay Deragon, Top 50 over 50 Global Marketing Thought Leaders*

The convergence of physical place with digital experience through our human data is poised to transform not only business, but also culture and society. Kate O'Neill digs into these layers and provides us with a far-reaching inquiry into the changes ahead in every industry for marketing, design, and technology.

— *Faisal Hoque, founder of Shadoka and other companies and author of several books including Everything Connects: How to Transform and Lead in the Age of Creativity, Innovation and Sustainability*

Kate O'Neill's Pixels and Place is a must read for those of us fascinated by the tidal shift taking place around us in the way we envision the world and our experiences within it.

— *Mitch Lowe, startup advisor, CEO of MoviePass, former president of RedBox, and a founding executive of Netflix*

PIXELS

AND

PLACE

Connecting Human Experience
Across Physical and Digital Spaces

by
Kate O'Neill

Also by Kate O'Neill

Lessons from Los Gatos: How Working at a Startup Called Netflix Made Me a Better Entrepreneur (and Mentor)

Surviving Death: What Loss Taught Me About Love, Joy, and Meaning

Acknowledgements

Thank you to everyone who has helped me research, has engaged in endless discussions about meaning and place, and put up with my obsessing over the topics. Big thanks to Sumit Shringi for designing such a wonderful cover. Huge thanks to my editor, Jocelyn Bailey, for her keen eye, the insights she contributed, and her positivity. And an enormous thank you to Robbie Quinn, my photographer and now my husband, whose work I use on the back cover and "About the Author" page, who makes every place more meaningful for me.

_____ orgia, who was my earliest introduction to both of the titular ideas in this book:

a curiosity about computers, and, through her tireless work within our Chicago-area hometown, the value of community and what a place can really mean.

A note on my use of the generic gender-neutral singular pronoun "they"

Throughout this book, as I describe scenarios involving unspecified actors, instead of the arbitrary use of a single gendered pronoun in generic use, whether "he" or "she," instead of the clunky "he/she" or wordy "he or she," and instead of painstakingly alternating between the uses of gendered pronouns, I have adopted the use of the singular "they." It was the American Dialect Society's 2015 word of the year, and it reflects a trend toward more inclusive language. Just like the convergence of pixels and place, you'll get used to it.

"When you tug at a single thing in the universe, you find it's attached to everything else."
— John Muir

"All models are false but some are useful."
— George E. P. Box

"Careful. We don't want to learn from this."
— Bill Watterson, Calvin and Hobbes

CHAPTER ONE

A Call to Action

I intend this book as a treatise, a manifesto of sorts, a call to action for anyone who designs experiences—in retail, healthcare, cities, in marketing of all kinds, and so on.

It is framed in the examination of pixels and place—of the convergence of our physical and digital surroundings, experiences, and even identities—because our future is beckoning us forward with little distinction between these layers of our reality, and we need to understand fully what it means to be human within that context. But the underlying message goes further: We need to understand *context* when we design experiences, because so many experiences—so many web forms, so many stores, so many services—are presented as if they exist in neatly contained isolation, where every person encountering them is in an identical place and mindset, on an identical screen, when the opposite of that is increasingly true.

This is not just about design for mobile or design for differing screen sizes, although that discussion belongs within the scope of our consideration; this is about recognizing that your brand or offering may be consumed on a laptop today, a phone tomorrow, then on a watch, then by voice command, and perhaps eventually as a passive service prompted by sensory cues needing only the bare minimum of interactions with the human consuming it. This is not a distant future vision; these interfaces and non-interfaces exist today, and their adoption by brands runs the gamut from bleeding-edge to blissfully ignorant. The bleeding-edge are risking and spending a great deal to understand the emerging possibilities, but the blissfully ignorant are taking risks, too:

They risk the possibility of becoming out of step with widespread cultural understanding of how digital experiences mesh with our physical surroundings, and eventually, if the brands continue to ignore the trends, they risk irrelevance.

For years I've been quoting the Peter Drucker line, "The aim of marketing is to know and understand the customer so well that the product or service fits [them] and sells itself."[1] Attendees of my workshops and speeches could bet that they'll hear this quote at some point during my presentations. But Drucker was alive and writing at a time when "knowing the customer" meant using good judgment, conducting surveys, and employing research techniques that generally got as specific as postal codes. Drucker wasn't speaking of using the finely detailed mesh of people's search histories, social statuses, social graphs, location tracking, and possibly their email archives as input to research. I can't speak for what he would have made of it, but I hope he might have had something sensible to say that reminded organizations to design systems with intention that could maximize the purpose of the business. I assume he'd still be asking the same big questions he always asked: What is your mission? Who is your customer? What does your customer value? What are your results? What is your plan?[2]

It's not clear what Drucker might have said about big data, connected devices, the Internet of Things, and consumer privacy, but what is clear is that we're in an age when these considerations are staring business leaders right in the face. What leaders decide to do with all of it will set a precedent for business in coming years. The generations that follow ours will live with the consequences of whether we built disciplined processes for ourselves and created compelling and meaningful experiences for the humans we interact with, or gave in to the allure of ever-more data and ever-greater invasions of privacy.

The best way for marketing to "know the customer" now is to truly function as a knowledge center, iterating through efforts to connect with customers, optimizing for insight, seeking to create more meaningful relationships with customers by getting clearer and clearer about what different people value for different reasons.

We need a framework for meaningful experience creation in a world where our personal data is collected invisibly as we pass through our physical surroundings. We need a model for marketing that can be effective without being creepy, to help companies succeed by being relevant and helpful. And we need a mindset to make responsible decisions with each other's data because we recognize the humanity it represents, and in doing so, make our possible future together a little bit brighter.

Pixels and Place . . . and People

How vividly do you remember the home you grew up in?

For most of us, our earliest sense of place was a home. We have sense memories of the sights and sounds, the smells of a kitchen, the feel of a carpet, and the stories and experiences assigned to that place. Those formative experiences may shape our understanding of the idea of "home" for the rest of our lives.

Home is a good place to start our journey, too, because it's a qualitative idea that overlays a physical place, rooted in the experience of that place, and it's an idea with which we all have at least one association. There are others: "Away." "In transit." "Work." Each term describes a concept that may equate to a particular place or movement through place, or it may be more of a loose idea associated with our experiences. For many of us, "school" encompasses both the building or campus where we were educated, as well as the overarching experience of our time at that institution and our relationships there.

In the last few decades, another place has risen to great importance in our everyday lives: "online." The word *online* describes a digital place, of sorts, or a series of places, but it is also rooted in the experience of those places. More and more of our time and attention is spent online, and our relationships are increasingly transacted in that realm.

From the outset of the internet, the metaphors we used to describe online space were borrowed from the physical world: pages, traffic, entries and exits, and so on. Even "home" page. But the distinction between "online" and "offline," between "digital" and "physical," once seemingly unambiguous, has begun to blur thanks to the ubiquity of smartphones and personal location data, ad and experience targeting, connected devices, wearable technology, the Internet of Things, and additive capabilities like 3-D printing. The meaningful design of experiences in physical space now regularly overlaps with the meaningful design of experiences in digital space.

But most experiences are not yet being designed with that awareness. And these experiences increasingly feel stiff and archaic—even anachronistic—compared to those that are.

Retail brands, cities, service companies, educational institutions, healthcare facilities, museums, and more have tremendous opportunities at this moment. Most aren't doing anything smart about this convergence of experience. The ones who do truly stand out, and they move us toward an understanding of what our future lives may look like as these blended experiences of pixels and place become more common. Indeed, the biggest opportunities for innovation, for profit, and for moving culture forward are going to emerge from integrating the layers intentionally, with an awareness of the metaphors we use to understand our experiences, a discipline about the data we collect, and a respect for the humanity that ties it all together.

> The biggest value and gains from the convergence of our digital lives and our physical surroundings will come from designing intentionally for a meaningful human experience.

Because human experience is the connective layer between the two realms—as our trackable interactions and transactions create the data stream that describes either space—the human experience needs to be designed with respect and intention.

What do I mean by "human experience" and human experience design? I think human experience is the natural successor to the narrower ideas of customer experience, user experience, patient experience, etc.— all of which point to a common need to understand, with equal parts empathy and strategic business-savvy, a person's ideal path in interacting with a company, brand, product, or service.

Even the concept of service design, while more closely aligned with the principles of being holistic, comprehensive, and integrated, is still slightly askew because the nomenclature subtly suggests a company-centric orientation. Company-centrism isn't hard to find; it's all throughout corporate culture and our work processes. If we want to be customer-centric, we have to risk overshooting ever so slightly. So let's say we're designing for human experience, making sure our business objectives—the experiences of our service or brand—mesh with what will be meaningful for the humans with whom we want to interact.

Within this book I present a framework for what a meaningful experience is—especially the experience of a place or space—so that human experience can be designed to be meaningful, with intention. When I'm describing concepts at this framework level, I'll call it Integrated Human Experience Design.

What to expect from this book

We have a lot to cover.

Throughout this book, I will examine the lessons for human experience designers on either side of the blurry divide. Since a great deal of the ground we'll cover relies on a shared understanding of abstractions, I'll define and explore the breadth and depth of concepts like experience, place, and meaning, to clarify what we're trying to build.

We'll visit the notion of placemaking, and how architects, city planners, and designers work to create a sense of culture, identity, and belonging in a building or urban development. We'll explore ideas about the cultivation of place, whether it's a city, a store, a college, a venue, or even a place that's as conceptual as it is real, like Wall Street, Music Row, or Hollywood.

We'll look closely at metaphor, and how much of the language we use in describing digital experience has been informed by physical phenomena, as well as the endless dimensions of meaning and associations these metaphors carry, especially in connected experiences.

For history and context, we'll look at some of the trends that brought us to this point, as well as at some of the possibilities the future may hold.

We'll even examine some of the elements that are common to the successful and meaningful design of integrated human experiences to give you tools and thought-starters about how to approach your projects.

Finally, we'll explore some of the patterns and practices of experience creation in physical and digital space across industries and disciplines, and discover how all of us—architects, designers, and strategists of landscape and information, retailers, restaurateurs, and more—can learn from each other.

The Opportunity

We all know elaborate scenarios from science fiction, where physical surroundings adapt themselves in our presence based on our data. Yet the reality isn't far off. Making some of these stories into reality is just a matter of integrating the data points.

The data points aren't easy to integrate, though, sometimes by design. We don't necessarily want the details of our life as a patient to cross over into the details of our life as a shopper or a traveler or a diner or a homeowner, and so on. Yet the conveniences some crossover could offer us are fairly undeniable.

Many of us make the choice to give up our personal information in exchange for convenience, or access to something interesting. The bargain we make is: "As long as you keep my data safe, you can have it; and you can make me offers that may entice me to spend my money on you, thus paying off whatever value you initially gave me." That's been at the heart of both the "freemium" model (previously known as the "shareware" model) and the free trial model (or, as some call it, the drug pusher's model where the "first one's free") for quite some time.

What's changing is that every service is collecting its own set of rich data. Some of it becomes publicly available, such as the data "firehose" (note the metaphor borrowed from the physical world) of tweets on Twitter, or the check-ins firehose on Foursquare. This data can be harvested, mined, cross-referenced, and targeted back to us with location awareness; and while the possibilities are exciting, they also can be terrifying for people. At the very least, it can be off-putting when a company reveals the source of their data too overtly.

We all spend our lives in roles—as employees, as consumers, as users, as patients, as students—and we know there are disconnects between them. That's what's happening here: There's a disconnect between the data we're giving up, and the opportunities we're not being given in exchange. There's a disconnect between what we think could be happening to make our lives easier and more fulfilled, and what mostly isn't happening.

Then there's the physical realm in which we live and move, and the digital realm in which we spend time, energy, and money—and there are arbitrary gaps between them. Within these gaps are opportunities for meaningful interaction that haven't been developed yet. (There are also opportunities to overreach people's trust and comfort levels, but we'll get into that as we go.)

I work with enough large, well-established companies to know that few have this figured out. In my consulting work with top retail and food brands and with leading universities, I see every client struggling to put the pieces in place, to make sense of the data they're collecting, and to make it meaningful in the context of their digital presence and physical spaces. And I see a lot of the other extreme, too: They aren't collecting the data they could be, which would give them the visibility they need to improve their business *and* the customer's experience.

So we, as strategists, designers, marketers, entrepreneurs, and anyone who creates experiences for a living, need to be mindful of our opportunity to make the most of this moment in time and not be left behind. Most companies may not have figured this out for themselves, but the ones that do will soar ahead in the coming years. The public's expectations will adjust. Integrating these experiences will soon become table stakes in business.

Who Is This Written For?

I think I recognize you: You're responsible for building a business. Maybe you're a marketing executive; maybe you're an entrepreneur. You're smart, you've done well, and you want to stay current on technology trends. At heart, you might be a salesperson or a strategist; either way, you read articles every day about the Internet of Things, big data, artificial intelligence, and so on, and you know there's something big going on.

What I want you to know going forward is that this is about your work and your business, but it's also about your family and your friends. And *you*: your data, your activities. Everyone is affected by the trends in this book. I want us to have a conversation about this. Picture your mom or dad or sister or brother or son or daughter, and imagine companies monitoring and analyzing their activities so that they can sell them more stuff. On some level, of course, it happens in so many ways we're inured to it; but it's important that we really step back and consider that.

I'm not here to say that analytics are bad. I'm here to say that analytics are human. Or at least, they represent the real needs and genuine interests of actual human beings; they're proxies for people. And as such, we are honor bound to be respectful with them, to consider them with nuance and care, to let them guide us toward creating experiences of delight or at least outcomes that fulfill mutual needs, not to use them, manipulate them, and exploit them.

> I'm not here to say that analytics are bad. I'm here to say that analytics are human.

The integration of online and offline experience through our personal data truly affects us all, but business leaders are in the best positions to make ethical and responsible decisions in how they use our data. So I'm primarily writing this for you, leaders at larger companies, cities, and institutions, since you are the ones who decide what will be allowed and what won't. You are the ones who determine the allocation of resources to designing for brand experience. You want your companies to be successful, and you also want to create something of value for the people who buy and use your products and services. I've helped many companies achieve those integrated objectives, and I want the same for you.

I see you, too, brand designers. You want your work to resonate. And you, information architects, strategists, and marketers, who want to develop effective and relevant products and services. I thought about those of you working in retail, healthcare, education, and entertainment, and there's something for each of you here. During my school years, my mother rose to become CEO of a chamber of commerce that served five of our neighboring communities, and I spent many of my formative years helping her organize events that connected small business owners with civic leaders and planners. So believe me, I thought a lot about you, local leaders and placemakers, and I have pulled together insights and knowledge that can help you. And I definitely remembered you, entrepreneurs. You want your product or service to have the greatest impact and potential, and there's a great deal to gain from the framework and the various industry patterns I've outlined.

This book is not so much written for the average layperson, although of course they're welcome to read it. This book is really about the fact that companies are *going* to collect people's data, and we need to talk about why it's important to think about human rights and customer rights and privacy as they're collecting customer data. We need to think not only about the effectiveness of our projects and our campaigns, but also about the future our projects are building. We need to envision what that world will look like for our kids and grandkids.

Calling my fellow Corporate Idealists

Years ago, I started a blog called Corporate Idealist, dedicated to the idea that business could be a creative and meaningful endeavor. I got to interview exemplary leaders like Tony Hsieh, CEO of Zappos, and along the way I collected and chronicled ideas about fostering a respectful culture for employees and a meaningful relationship with customers. I managed the blog for about a year, bringing in collaborators, sponsors, and a steady following of readers who shared the vision and wanted inspiration to do it right. The whole experience of building a community of people who wanted to focus on the value in business left me with the strong sense that people want their work to matter, and they want to do the right thing.

Business isn't only about making money. A corporations is, by nature; but humans are the ones doing the work (for now), and by our nature we need more purpose than that. So for us, it's about creating something of value, and building out that value through interaction with people. My belief is that there is a subculture in business of the people who recognize the opportunity to create value. These people are interested in being rewarded for their work and their ideas, but they're also interested in building something great.

In short, if your work involves designing, developing, or delivering an experience to people, whether online or offline (but *especially* if you do both), you will want to think about this integrated approach.

Organizational implications of integrating experiences

A consequence of this integration of online and offline experiences is the organizational implication in business that if you hire or bring in a human experience design role or consultant, the scope of that role needs to supersede the increasingly arbitrary distinctions of "online" and "offline" in order to be effective. I'm thinking specifically of the architects of digital place: user experience professionals, strategists, designers, marketers, or anyone who is engaged in the business of making a digital landscape more people-friendly. As strategist Chris Buettner writes:

> To create exceptional place-based digital experiences, you need wizards in architecture, technology, storytelling, experience design, engineering, and data science. When done well, the resulting fusion connects, inspires, and immerses us in ways that other types of digital experiences can't. [3]

It's difficult to separate marketing from user experience, and user experience from information architecture, and information architecture from data science, and data science from marketing. And content strategy, and branding, and front end design, and web development, and operations, and so on. Around and around it goes. These fields overlap because in practice, they must all integrate seamlessly to create meaningful, memorable, effective, and ultimately profitable customer experiences.

CHAPTER TWO

Defining the Undefinable: Place, Experience, and How We Create Meaning

If we're going to create meaningful human experiences through the integration of our digital and physical lives, we need to clarify what constitutes an experience, and what makes it meaningful.

Experience

The definition of *experience* has to be broad.

For our purposes, let's say that in marketing and design terms, *experience* is **any of a set of perceptions or interactions a person has with an entity**, which could be a brand, a place, or even another person.

The term has to be used that broadly because we have to encompass many possibilities.

Place

Place is almost more complicated to define than *experience*.

There's the idea of place as a geographical area—a location with boundaries either explicit or loosely understood.

There's place as part of identity, which is an important facet of urban planning and urban design. Anyone who follows discussions on the development and redevelopment of cities is familiar with the ways in which place-based identity is invoked.

There's place as in "sense of place," an esoteric characteristic that a place may have, perceptible to many or to one. This idea is something Yi-Fu Tuan has explored.[4] If a place lacks a sense of place, it may be described as placeless or inauthentic.

As a side note, isn't it interesting how place can refer to social position or rank, as in "knowing one's place"?

For the sake of simplicity, where the place is more a shared, communal experience, I'll talk about communities associated with a place. Where the place is more a private, entity-owned experience, usually driven by profit, I'll talk about the "owners" of that place. These usages are bound to be blurry, though. Privately-owned spaces intended for the public fall into a gray area, such as zoos or even government-managed squares and parks. But we'll do the best we can.

Meaning, and Why It Matters Here

The world is full of noise, and we are constantly struggling to make sense of it.

From the busyness of our daily lives, we seek clarity of purpose that can help us better understand our priorities. Amid the chaos of the marketing messages we receive, we seek alignment with our existing needs and motivations.

What do we even mean by *meaning*?

Meaning in this case has depth and dimensions of significance, relevance, connection to purpose. It's what matters. There are many ideas related to meaning in its many variations: alignment, mindfulness, intention, fulfillment, holism, happiness, contentment, resilience, and many more. If we want to create effective, even transcendent experiences, we need to understand the nature of what is meaningful. And to do that we need to understand a bit of the multifaceted nature of meaning.

There are fundamental ways that meaning informs our lives and work, if we are conscious of it and recognize its shape. The shape *meaning* takes in **marketing** is *empathy*: All relevant customer understanding and communications flow from being aware of and aligned with the customer's needs and motivations. In **business** in a broader sense, the shape *meaning* takes is *strategy*. It guides every decision and action. In

technology and data science, *meaning* can drive the pursuit of *applied knowledge* toward that which improves our experiences and our lives. Creative work becomes more meaningful the more it conveys truth. And **in our lives overall**, an understanding of what is meaningful to us provides us with *purpose, clarity, and intention.*

To consider meaning at any level implies a search for the depth and dimensions of what is significant, what truly matters. How any given decision relates to a larger purpose. To consider meaning at a communications level is to ponder relevance. Meaning at an existential level surfaces what brings fulfillment, happiness, or contentment. Meaning in our lives fosters resilience.

> To consider meaning at any level implies a search for the depth and dimensions of what is significant, what truly matters.

Meaning is clearly a vast subject with lots of layers. But the more rigorous our thinking about it is, the more clearly we can communicate our intentions and achieve our objectives.

In terms of the relationship between brand and consumer, the need for meaning goes both ways, underlying both the corporate/brand-centric world and the humanistic/consumer-centric world. From a marketer's perspective, we need to find meaningful patterns in the data we collect, or there's no point in collecting it. A framework that determines what is likely to be most meaningful is important before we ever embark on campaigns and data collection.

The role of meaning in the integrated design of physical and digital experiences is at once a technological question, because of the integration, and a marketing question, because of the design. The technology and integration parts of the equation, due to their relationship to applied knowledge, aren't likely to cause resistance. But I often hear feedback from people that marketing and design imply a level of control, of one party exerting influence over another.

So it's worth noting, in thinking about meaning in marketing, that for all the knocks on marketing as a profession, there are moments when something that is genuinely a force for good, or at least a force for joy, is able to connect with more people as a result of some clear alignment and relevance. To accomplish that kind of meaningful marketing still requires segmentation and strategy and messaging and all the other tools and disciplines of marketing overall. So the tools can't tell us anything about merit; those are shared by everything from noble causes to sleazy scams. Merit can only be assessed by the objectives and the outcome.

To achieve the meaningful and memorable integrated experiences we strive for requires a sincere effort to reconcile the capabilities of technology with the insights of marketing. Anything short of true partnership between these areas will ring hollow.

Meaning follows us and morphs from role to role in our lives. We are our professional selves, where we intentionally create interactions with others, just as we are ourselves in our roles as consumers, users, patients, guests, students, visitors, and so on; we have our own aspirations and motivations, and these guide our actions. The entities that engage with us do well to recognize and respect our life journeys independent of our interactions with those entities; otherwise their messages and their offerings fall flat.

In my estimation, there is no question that we stand to benefit societally, individually, and within our businesses by paying more attention to the layers of meaning.

How We Make Meaning

There's a premise I learned while studying linguistics in grad school that I have since found applies in a useful way to marketing, and generally to creating experiences. The idea is that, fundamentally, there are three parts of communication: what the speaker intended, the message itself, and what the listener received.

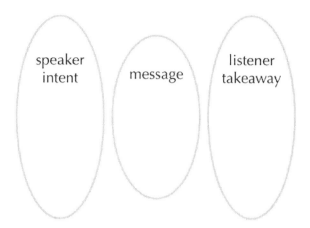

The overlap between these three components is where shared understanding has been communicated. It could be said this is where the meaning is.

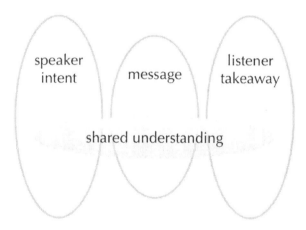

There's another facet worth considering, though, and that's context. In what context does the communication take place? How much shared history did the speaker and listener have to begin with? What was the nature of their relationship, and how much does this message build on their previous attempts to communicate?

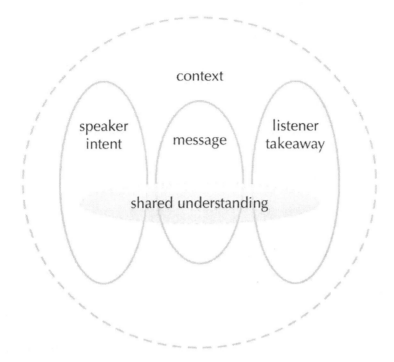

That last part is important when we apply this model to marketing or any communication that takes place online. So much of the quality of how the customer or user receives the message has to do with the context of that interaction, much of which has to do with where they are physically: what their physical capabilities and limitations are in terms of, say, the device they're using, and so on. This takes us right back to the importance of place.

The Intentional Design of Human Experience

The integrated world is coming at us fast and furious. Connected devices and always-on data sharing are becoming the norm, and the ways we as consumers interact with the "built environment" and the ways we as experience designers build that environment are becoming increasingly multifaceted and complex.

You can tell this is true by how many terms there are to describe the work that relates to this field: user experience, customer experience, service design, usability, interaction design, content strategy, information architecture, and so on.

These terms and the job functions they describe have mostly been around for twenty years or more, but they have been evolving rapidly in recent years and are still evolving, perhaps even more rapidly. It's never all that easy to talk about one without invoking some of the others; there's considerable overlap between them in terms of the skills practitioners have in these fields, the objectives they seek to fulfill, and the output they produce. But there are subtle differences between the focus of each of these kinds of design, and it's worth clarifying them.

Bear in mind that any time one steps into the field of semantics, one is risking quibbles over minutiae. After all, we're discussing subtleties that are subjective to some extent, perhaps colored by the specific definitions in use in specific environments. So the way I describe these disciplines is only in contrast to the usefulness of the idea of "human experience" and is not intended to be a definitive summary of each discipline. They're all useful in their own respects.

User experience (or UX, as it's often abbreviated) is primarily concerned with on-screen interactions—as the name suggests, circumstances in which a person is the "user" of a product or service. It differs from service design primarily in scope: It is not typically thought to encompass holistic, online/offline interactions, although it will no doubt increasingly have to do so.

Customer experience (CX) deals with elements of the brand that pertain to the purchase path, from beginning to end or ongoing. It is human-centric in the sense that it characterizes interactions around the motivations of the person who is acting as a customer; but in framing the person as a "customer," it centers the person's role in terms of their interaction with the company, and tends to ignores their life journey apart from the customer-specific touchpoints they may have. This limitation is helpful in framing the scope of the tools and methodologies, but CX can overlook meaningful moments in the person's life that bring them to a point of considering relevant purchases.[5]

As an aside, the analyst firm Gartner has predicted that by 2017, 50 percent of consumer product investments will be redirected to customer experience innovations.[6] So this category is certainly understood as

17

valuable.

There are more—such as service design, interaction design, user interface design, usability, and so on. Every one of these disciplines is valuable and important, but for the purposes of discussing a holistic approach to designing integrated experiences for humans without bringing over any implicit preconceived notions about how to do that, throughout this book I'll continue to talk about human experience and human experience design.

Moreover, I want to step away from framing the human beings we interact with as users or customers only. The opportunity to look holistically at people's lives and their surroundings can open up possibilities to align our organizations' motives with the motives of the people who engage with us. If you operate within user experience, customer experience, interaction design, or any other related discipline, you can always apply the tools of your trade to the issues presented here to solve the challenges of integrated experience in a way that works for you.

Experience and Meaning

If we want to understand how to use meaning to frame our strategy and approach, and if we want to reliably create meaningful experiences, we have to think beyond how we *perceive* meaning and think more deeply about how we *make* meaning.

For experiences to resonate, they need to have meaning. And in order to understand what people really experience when they interact with brands, products, devices, and so on, we'll need an understanding of the framework of meaning. "Meaning as framework" in this sense will include: what message is intentionally or unintentionally being conveyed; the metaphors and mechanisms being used; in what context the message exists; and what lasting impressions that experience leaves.

The Wikipedia entry for *experience* points out that "the word 'experience' may refer, somewhat ambiguously, both to mentally unprocessed immediately perceived events as well as to the purported wisdom gained in subsequent reflection on those events or interpretation of them."[7] I love that overlapping definition. The more experiences (events) a person goes through, the more experience (wisdom) they have.

In a parallel way, meaning has not only multiple meanings—semantic, intentional, existential, cosmic, and that's skipping quite a few—but also meanings that layer upon each other, even within the scope of marketing. The more *meaning* a brand message is able to convey to a customer, the more *meaning* the interaction has, and the more it aligns with the customer's *meaning* in the broadest sense. I don't know if you caught it on the first read-through, but if not, try looking again: Those are three different levels of meaning.

It's useful, too, to think of this kind of layering taking place as you design experiences. Everything that a customer encounters, from hearing about a company through word of mouth, to purchasing a product, all the way through maintenance issues and service interactions, and eventually through repurchase or abandonment—all of these are experience points or potential experience points.

Each of those interactions—those *experiences*—between a person and a brand entity contributes to the person's overall perspective of, or *experience* with, that entity.

In marketing and in experience design, meaning is a dimension of experience. It occurs where purpose and value are aligned in the transaction. Experiences can be meaningful on a variety of levels: how well it fulfills a given intention or purpose, how well it aligns with what a person values, how memorable it is, how lasting an impact it has on a person, and so on.

We need these layered and interdependent definitions of experience and meaning, because we need the context that reminds us that the immediate interactions we design for our users and customers contribute to a larger collected sense of the brand. We also need to be reminded that there are implications of meaning within data, both in terms of how we look at data meaningfully (as in how it informs our decisions and interactions) and how we see meaning in data (as in how we recognize patterns that tell us if people value what we're doing).

Because if analytics are people, as I stated early on, it stands to reason that transactions are relationships. The macro view of the relationship helps foster a sense of accountability in the micro. And when we're dealing with people's personal and sensitive data, we need to be reminded of that accountability.

Also, in the age of social media, memorable experiences tend to be shareable experiences. If you offer me a remarkable moment, whether visually, emotionally, or otherwise, I'm likely to share it. If the remarkableness translates, it's likely to be re-shared. Word of mouth marketing, of course, is strong advocacy for a brand, so these remarkable/re-shareable experiences are the benchmark to which we're all aspiring.

There's a range of ways to accomplish a memorable connection with your intended audience, and they range from both low-technology to high-technology and from low context awareness to high context awareness.

The technology actually matters less than the context. Consider a low-tech but context-aware outreach mechanism, like billboards on the side of a country road with message fragments that only make sense in succession as you see each one. There's nothing high-tech about it, but it's very in tune with the context of the majority of its viewers, and because of that shared context, it stands a good chance of being memorable. It isn't necessarily *more* important to be memorable than relevant, but consider that a memorable message is still memorable even when it *isn't* relevant, and it is certainly memorable when it *is* relevant.

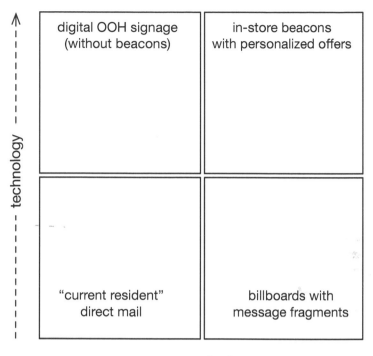

In terms of memorability and differentiation, we also talk about the *experience economy*, which is a term that's been in use for almost twenty years. Coined by Pine and Gilmore, the term pertains to differentiating the experience of the brand.[8] Examples include Starbucks, Walt Disney, Nordstrom, and many more.

The term and idea has taken on new depth with the rise of the "sharing economy," with companies like Uber, Airbnb, and so on competing for market share in an access versus ownership model based on differentiated experiences. (See the section on "Ownership Versus Access and Privately-Owned Public Spaces.")

The goal in any case is to decrease friction, to make things easier—but easier in a way that moves people naturally toward an outcome they'll enjoy and from which the company will benefit. That's the best chance of achieving meaning in experience.

Your customer is happily going about life, and you're happily going about your business, when suddenly your paths cross. Your customer's needs meet yours. It's an interaction, and an *opportunity* for meaningful interaction.

When people talk about what is meaningful to them, they often say that it "matters." "To matter" implies a certain level of importance, perhaps even cosmic importance, or at least contextual importance. More to the point, it implies a certain alignment with purpose.

That's perhaps the easiest way to distill what makes something (especially an experience, in this case) meaningful: the ease with which it fits into our idea of purpose and aligns with what is relevant to us.

The key here, from a marketing perspective, is: It isn't meaningful if it only fulfills your purpose. It likewise isn't meaningful if it only fulfills your customer's purpose. A meaningful experience is one that fulfills an intersecting set of purposes in alignment.

So the more crisp your understanding of your purpose is (see more about this in the section on "Intentionality, or Purpose"), and the more disciplined you are about how to follow through with it, the more effectively you can measure your efforts toward achieving meaningfulness —which may be all you really need.

Senses in Place; Sense and Technology

During my last year as an undergraduate, I lived in an off-campus apartment in Chicago's Little Italy with two roommates above an Italian restaurant. When I think back to that time and place, what almost always comes to mind first is the pungent but pleasant smell of garlic roasting every morning as the kitchen prepared food for the day. What's more, when I smell roasting garlic, I often find myself thinking about that apartment.

Our sensory input about a place is a key part of how we experience the place, what we associate with it, what we remember about it, and ultimately what the place *means* to us.

We have a lot of bandwidth for processing visual information, as popularized in a TED Talk by David McCandless about data visualization. Basing his talk on the work of Danish physicist Tor Nørretranders, McCandless explained:

> He converted the bandwidth of the senses into computer terms . . .
> Your sense of sight is the fastest. It has the same bandwidth as a
> computer network. Then you have touch, which is about the speed of
> a USB key. And then you have hearing and smell, which has the
> throughput of a hard disk. And then you have poor old taste, which is
> like barely the throughput of a pocket calculator. And . . . 0.7 percent,
> that's the amount we're actually aware of.[9]

Our senses help us create meaning. Our sense of sight clearly takes in a lot of data fast, and we process a lot of the world that way. What we see is a big part of what we think we know. What we hear is even more of it.

It stands to reason that sensory stimuli offer big opportunities for design.

Touch is, of course, a big part of interface design. The kinesthetic sense is often overlooked, but this includes gesture, which is a big part of emerging interface design, too.

And then there's extrasensory perception: what we seem to be aware of, but we can't identify. How does this intuition figure into how we go through connected space? On the other hand, how much of what we think of as intuition is actually our kinesthetic sense?

Our kinesthetic sense, and how it encompasses movement through space and place, is part of our larger framework of meaning-making. It's a very relevant piece of our framework in considering the overlay of technology on place. That overlay has brought us GPS and Google Maps among many other innovations, yet have you ever wondered whether using Google Maps inhibits our sense of direction and our ability to navigate on our own?

Several studies have indeed shown that using GPS diminishes our ability to reconstruct the directions we took to get from place to place. Separate studies have also shown that the "ego-centric" experience of GPS mapping, when the map re-orients based on one's location, leads to fewer mistakes for the navigator in getting where they're going; but it also diminishes the navigator's ability to recall landmarks they passed to get there. (See also the section on "Humanlike Nuances" for an example of an app that gives directions like a human would.)

Does that mean we shouldn't use on-demand mapping? Or does it imply an opportunity to develop a new kind of navigation experience that might empower us with the confidence of accurate navigation while letting us stay connected—or connecting us more deeply—with our surroundings? This is where thinking about the meaning of a person's experience can lead us to wonderful possibilities. For example, what if you could get directions and optionally turn on a program that would give you architectural history as you walked? What if you had a rough day and wanted a prettier drive home from work?

> "Why don't we offer the choice to go slow, to take the least polluted route to work, or the scenic way home?"
> —Marcus Foth[10]

This is also where augmented reality has the chance to shine.

Think back to video games that forced the player to navigate top-down in the game's place, like Pac-Man. The rise in popularity of what are known as "first-person shooter" and other first-person perspective games creates an expectation of feeling immersed in the game's world. It's the perfect set of training wheels for an integrated experience environment that involves augmented and virtual reality, which we'll explore further in the chapter "Augmented Reality Games."

Cues, Triggers, and Metaphors: Sensory Experience Design

Since we know that our senses help us make meaning, we can recognize how placemakers in the physical world have long used sensory cues to establish certain associations for customers and visitors. These are common in retail and tourism, among other industries.

Whole Foods and the experience of "fresh"

Martin Lindstrom wrote in *Brandwashed* that Whole Foods is a great example of "priming." Their fine control of sensory cues throughout the store signals "freshness" and evokes the folksiness of farmers' markets.[11]

The entrance for most grocery stores opens right into the produce section, but upon entering a Whole Foods store, the shopper is greeted with racks of cut flowers—not because they're the highest-margin items, but because they symbolize freshness. Imagine if the first thing you saw when you walked into the store was a big stack of canned tuna. (Or a display of plastic flowers.)

Within the produce department, the shopper encounters not only display walls of produce, but large islands in the center of the aisle featuring stacked-up wooden crate displays of seasonal produce, like something like you might see at a farmers' market.

And like many grocery stores, they spray produce with a mist of water, suggesting crops in a field, even though, ironically, it appears this actually makes them rot faster. But no matter: The fine mist gives the appearance of freshness.

Disney and the multisensory experience

Disney theme parks are masterful with multisensory marketing with scent—where certain rides or areas of the park have distinct associated smells, like Pirates of the Caribbean and its slight mustiness, or like Main Street USA with its vanilla—and with audio reinforcement of beloved (and/or annoying) childhood songs. Castle mock-ups even have small entrances to make visitors feel larger-than-life.

But now technologies like wearables and 3-D printing are rich with possibilities for both physical placemakers as well as for the digital design of "place." In 2014, Disney made a billion-dollar investment in MyMagic +, a "next-generation technology-fueled customer experience that transforms the way its guests play, stay, and pay at the 'most magical place on Earth.'"[12]

You can use the Disney World app to reserve not only a table but also your whole meal at a restaurant called Be Our Guest. If you're wearing your Disney MagicBand when you arrive for your reservation, you'll be greeted by name and invited to sit anywhere. And like magic, your pre-ordered food shows up to your table.

The MagicBands make use of long-range radio, with a transmission range of more than forty feet. They create a seamless experience from before the trip ever begins to after the trip concludes. They've made considerable efforts to contain and control every aspect of the experience.

Few brands would have as much control over their visitors' or customers' experience, but it's certainly worth considering how some of these ideas could help create meaning, and in turn create more meaningful relationships between customer and brand.

The Selfish Perk of Meaningfulness

I'd like to believe that everyone is motivated by the idea of offering something of value in the world and doing more meaningful work. But maybe you're not entirely convinced, or maybe your boss is not entirely convinced.

So here's where I tell you a big secret I've learned in my years of working with Fortune 500 companies as well as start-ups: Meaningful marketing is more effective marketing. Designing experiences from a human point of view rather than a company point of view leads to a greater chance of getting it right, and getting people to buy. Maybe without pushy and gimmicky tactics you miss a few people who would be gullible or weak, but those people were never going to be your fans anyway. They were never going to be truly happy with their purchase, and they were never going to recommend you to their friends.

After all, this is about your *relationship* with the person on the other side of the transaction. We don't have to pretend that there's not a profit motive for companies, but even from that standpoint, doing it right matters because it's expensive to acquire customers. Data collection is expensive. Paying marketers and designers and analysts is expensive, and you want them to have the best material to work with. Businesses can't afford the cost of being haphazard with experience design or sloppy with data collection; and they can't afford the risks that come with playing fast and loose with experiences created after data analysis.

Offering relevant messaging and experiences demonstrates a kind of respect for the person you're interacting with—your customer, user, whatever their role—and their interests, their time, their concerns, and so on. Delivering relevance while also walking the line of discretion, without creeping out the customer, is another part of that respect. Doing all this right breeds trust and loyalty.

Which, of course, ultimately pay off in profit for the company.

So it doesn't really matter which philosophy motivates you most. Both an altruistic passion for creating more meaningful experiences and a profit-centric drive end up in the same place: using data about and empathy for the context of the human you're interacting with to improve their experiences, and doing it with respect to relevance and discretion.

Your customers are researching you online, they're on your competitors' websites in your store, they're looking for contextual cues that you understand how their lives are increasingly both physical and digital. They're using apps to order coffee; they're using smart fitting rooms; they're posting pictures of your merchandise, your food, your waiting room online. The more you ignore that, the more you risk losing them to competitors who understand it and work with it.

For me, though, and maybe for you, the benefits of more meaningful experiences have as much to do with being engaged in my work, feeling good about what I do, and wanting to leave the world a little better, not a little worse.

Measuring Experiences Meaningfully

Part of the challenge is not just to measure, but to measure meaningfully.

In a city, it might be tempting to look at rising parking costs as an indicator of inaccessibility, whereas in another context, it might make more sense to evaluate a downtown's overall accessibility by how many means of getting there exist. Rising parking costs might be a healthy way to discourage people from driving into downtown, relying on higher volume public transportation instead.

Digital experiences and physical experiences alike tempt us with meaningless metrics. "Vanity" metrics like visits, followers, and likes aren't usually the best indicators of success. What we can take away from that into the physical environment is that the most obvious and superficially satisfying metrics won't necessarily be the ones that illustrate anything worthwhile or actionable.

To measure meaningful experiences, then, we need some sense of this framework, and a delta of someone's emotional state before and after they interacted or transacted with our brand or product.

On the low-tech side, surveys may be useful for this purpose. The closest proxies we have for meaningful measurement are things like satisfaction or Net Promoter Score. Which is fair: We can hypothesize that if someone finds an experience meaningful, they will likely be satisfied with it.

But other things can affect satisfaction, such as the relief one feels at the completion of an arduous task. That doesn't necessarily hint at the value that may have been created or transacted in the process.

More sensitive metrics are in development. Biochemical reactions can be tracked using wearables, and facial expressions that reveal mood and reaction can be determined using recognition algorithms. The opportunities for a much more accurate assessment of emotional state are increasingly possible.

CHAPTER THREE

Convergence and Integration

Did you ever imagine you'd be alive in a time when your refrigerator could do your grocery shopping? I didn't. Maybe I just didn't watch enough episodes of *The Jetsons* when I was growing up, but the convergence of connected technology with my physical surroundings has both surprised and delighted me.

But as a digital marketing consultant and advocate for meaningful human experiences online, I also hear frequently from clients and audiences that they're overwhelmed. And as anyone using these technologies knows, there's often a shortfall in delivering on the full promise of the opportunities this convergence creates.

It's not merely that we're falling short of marketing potential. It's that we're too often exploiting customer data in shortsighted and, frankly, greedy ways without fully considering that our own data will fall into that trap as the net grows wider. We have to be mindful of the precedent our work sets. It's hardly hyperbole to say that nothing short of the future of humanity depends on it.

So while we do have smart refrigerators and smart thermostats and smart clothes and smart cities and even smart toilets, and before long the mainstream use of driverless cars, we're falling down on building smart experiences into our own businesses. The lines between online and offline are blurring more and more, yet we often ignore the context of the user's physical environment or device limitations as we expect them to interact with our brands, our products, and our services. And too often we collect customer data we don't use, which could help create more relevant experiences.

Until recently our experience of physical space was pretty distinct from our understanding of digital space, but the connected landscape is blending the layers more and more. The online and offline worlds have increasing overlap, and that overlap happens *through us*, the human beings who experience it and whose experience of those worlds is tracked and mined.

Remember what an experience *is*. (As discussed in the earlier section, "Experience and Meaning.") For our purposes, it's any discernible interaction with or impression of an entity, a place, a brand, a person, or a community.

As we have these interactions just about everywhere the physical world and the digital world converge, the connective layer is the data captured through human experience. The key point here is that, much of the time, *we* are the pivot point through which these layers connect.

Let me say that again: Almost every one of the points where the physical world and digital world meet is through us.

Our human experience facilitates the bulk of the connections where the physical world meets the digital world. Our purchases and shopping patterns, our visits to our favorite websites from our favorite easy chairs, our obsession with tracking our steps and our other fitness data through wristbands and watches and phones and other wearables, our check-ins on social media, our location-tagged travel photos, our tracked movements via sensors, and more. So much more than we tend to think about; and all of it creates a data trail of our experiences.

Almost every one of the points where the physical world and digital world meet is through us.

Everything truly interesting about the Internet of Things is interesting because of how it affects our lives as humans. Even when you think about data that seems arcane or abstract and removed from human interactions, like the data around improving the operational efficiency of factories, or server logs in some government agency, or financial data from the depths of Wall Street, it's all still optimized for improving human lives in some way. It's only a step or two removed from human experience.

We use phones, watches, tablets, chatbots, voice command, and more to move through the world, provide for our needs, and control our surroundings. More and more our world is not divided into online and offline: We're simply ordering a coffee, listening to music, planning our route to a meeting, booking travel, making plans with friends. And more and more of these interactions need to move seamlessly from one mode to another and back again.

Two problems: First, the gatekeepers of experience—brands, cities, institutions, etc.—haven't necessarily kept up with expectations, so those interactions often *don't* flow seamlessly from one mode to another as they should. Second, these interactions and experiences are increasingly served up by algorithms as part of workflows that are subservient to revenue agendas and profit motives.

Now that's evil not in itself; it's just complicated. Profit motives introduce ethical dilemmas when it comes to protecting people, and when the data that tracks people's movements, behaviors, moods, preferences, habits, purchases, conversations, finances, and so on is involved, we definitely need to be concerned as a society about protecting people. For-profit healthcare has struggled with this duality: How can providers improve patient outcomes, increase their efficiency, and decrease costs, all while protecting patient data?

Now, because of data tracking, personalization, and integrated experiences, that dilemma is showing up in nearly every industry. How can you offer a timely, relevant experience that satisfies some human need or motivation, make money while doing it, and protect your customer's or user's data at the same time?

So our opportunity is to think humanistically about the way these are coming together—because these layers are converging in ways that are experimental and interesting and innovative, but not yet intentional about facilitating a more meaningful human experience.

And they need to be, because we are the ones at the center of them.

Balance Versus Integration

You know how people talk about "work-life balance"? The goal is to closely manage the time, attention, and energy you give to your work life so that your personal life can also benefit from your time, attention, and energy.

You've probably noticed that voices of wisdom often talk instead about work-life *integration*—when you make thoughtful choices about the design of your work life so that it enriches your personal life, and so that your personal life can help you achieve a more fulfilling work life. Work-life integration is also about making your overall life experience richer and more meaningful.

Similarly, we can each make intentional choices about integrating our physical and digital lives so that each will benefit the other.

But there's a limit to what any given individual can accomplish. We're dependent on the data models that surround us. We're dependent on the experiences that have been created for us in those spaces. The capacity for integration has to be more universally available; it has to be part of the design of our surroundings, part of the ecosystem we live in. When we think about designing a physical space, such as a retail store, or a hospital, or a university, or a public space in a city, we also need to be thinking about how the people who use this space will experience it as their other selves. What digital experiences will people have in that physical space? We should think about how to facilitate that digital experience and how to make those experiences seamless.

> The capacity for integration has to be universally available; it has to be part of the design of our surroundings, part of the ecosystem we live in.

All the while, let's keep in mind the very real needs of the human beings who have these interactions with us.

On the digital side, we can prepare for integration as we create e-commerce environments, or when creating online banking, or online healthcare services, or any website or any mobile app or any API or data system or really *anything* that is going to serve up a digital experience meant to be consumed by humans. We can develop digital systems in human-integrative ways by dismantling the monolith of the systems' perspective; instead, customer motivations and needs must drive system functions, and in turn each function of the system should blend as frictionlessly as possible with the likely physical environments and contexts that people may be in as they experience them.

A clothing brand and its e-commerce site, for example, can't expect every interaction to lead to purchase if they want to allow for more frictionless integration. They have to plan for customer curiosity, self-discovery, aspirational browsing, and so on, and each of these may take place just about anywhere.

After all, an integrative experience may not always be a meaningful one, but a disjointed experience is far less likely to ever be meaningful.

We make this effort knowing, of course, that the environments and contexts people are likely to be in will vary more and more all the time; we can't just think "mobile" and mentally substitute phones. Tablets and wearables like watches make up a substantial portion of people's on-the-go consumption, and those are two very different interfaces that complement very different usage scenarios and require a different set of data to interact appropriately with them. Integrated messaging and notifications may also have good reason to appear on screens and devices around us in our homes, our vehicles, our workplaces, and where we eat, shop, and visit. They may be reminders, alerts, and even offers, if they're genuinely relevant. But the data required to gauge how effective these integrative interactions are will differ: Whereas a notification displayed on a watch can rely on gesture feedback to optimize the experience—when the wearer turns their wrist to see the watch face—the data that can track the effectiveness of a notification on a digital display in a store may have to do with proximity.

Mind you, there's a very real risk of overstepping the line where people are most comfortable. No one wants to feel targeted, but most people do want to be shown an appropriate level of attention. If the interaction is integrative and respectful, it can be helpful and successful. If it's intrusive, irrelevant, compromising, or gimmicky, it will ultimately fail.

Perhaps the Golden Rule is the best way to think about all of this: the data we collect about others is going to be collected about us, too. The experiences we create for others will set the standards for the experiences others create for us. Overall, if we're mindful of how we design data-rich experiences, we can make those experiences more helpful, more enjoyable, more memorable, and more fulfilling.

Responsive Design and Integrated Human Experience Design

There's been a movement within web design over the last few years advocating for "responsive design": designing content that incorporates adaptive styling that adjusts appropriately when viewed on a range of screen sizes. Instead of having a "mobile version" of your website, for example, your content is simply your content, and it is prepared in such a way that the same content will work equally well on a 27-inch monitor and a 4.7-inch smartphone screen.

While that's not the same premise as designing with an awareness of the physical context someone is in—or agnosticism about their physical context, depending on how you look at it—there's certainly a related idea going on there. In the case of responsive design, the presentation of a digital experience allows for the possibility of multiple device contexts.

In Integrated Human Experience Design, the presentation of *any* experience, online or offline, allows for the possibility of multiple digital or physical contexts. In other words, if I'm designing a shopping experience that is primarily focused on the physical retail space, I must also be mindful of the digital interaction the customer will have with the store, and allow for nuanced opportunities to enrich the shopping experience through the integration of those layers.

Data Determines Success; You Determine the Data Model

There's always some benchmark for whether or not a project worked, or how well it worked, and at some point in a for-profit corporation that benchmark, ultimately, is bound to be profit. But there are meaningful measures of preliminary success well before interactions turn to profit, and usually they follow some sort of "funnel" model. Typically, the data points the company tracks relative to that funnel aren't customer-centric but rather company-centric, like the old standard: "awareness > consideration > preference > purchase." In almost every environment, some metric will be the benchmark of success in every meeting and every debrief of that project.

The data we collect about that project is, then, how we evaluate the project's success.

Here's the thing, though: You are (or someone you work with is) determining or helping to determine that data model. Which means there's a chance to define the success in terms of how the customer experiences it. Some companies are doing this, and taking a truly customer-led approach to defining the success of their brands.

Did the customer find what they were looking for? How do you know? Did the customer complete the task they came in to complete?

As I often say: Analytics are people. And relevance, in terms of offering targeted messages and experiences, is a form of showing respect for your customer's time and interests. So is discretion regarding their privacy. All of these principles are really about data practices.

We all know that companies are going to collect customer data, so I want to equip them with frameworks for doing it ethically, mindfully, meaningfully. We all know that companies are going use customer data to sell products and services; I want to help them do it in a way that centers humanity in the perspective.

It's important that you then have the mindset as you approach the data model that the data needs to be rich and relevant, and it needs to be humanistic and able to encompass the richness and rigor of the human experience.

CHAPTER FOUR

The Humanity in the Data

If you take nothing else away from this book, what I most want you to remember is that whenever you see website analytics, or customer data, or big data about health trends, or any other data that has to do with something human beings have bought, done, or said, you should stop and think about the humanity represented in that data.

That's it. That's my big goal.

In the many years I've worked with companies on their marketing strategies and digital analytics and user experience and so on, I've noticed how common it is for marketers, executives, designers, and even strategists to get caught up in the abstractions of the data, and forget that they're talking about real people. That conversion optimization is about getting more *people* to buy something—which is great, if what you're enticing them to buy has value to them. If you can find the people for whom the thing is valuable, you're doing them a service. If not, you're making the world a worse place. Don't make the world a worse place.

I have said, and often say, that analytics are people. And of course I know that's an oversimplification. There are plenty of analytics about server logs, manufacturing equipment, industrial machinery, and so on that appear to have nothing to do with people. But then again, don't they? Why else would we care about the efficiency of those servers, the output of that equipment, and the safety of that machinery if not for people? The key idea here is that what we measure, we typically measure because it makes our human lives better. And it's good to remember that.

We often hear experts advocating for empathy in the design process, but rarely do we hear about it in analysis. Marketing cycles of campaign and channel management bring with them a whole lot of access to consumer data, but unless the marketer is willing to see the data as a proxy for actual people, there's no empathy. Really, the more data a marketer has, the more empathy they should be able to feel . . . *if* they're correctly associating the data with the humanity on the other side.

The Data Layers that Connect the Physical and the Digital

Increasingly, our surroundings are created by actors we don't know are there. We can't see them, we probably don't understand them, and we have no control over them anyway. So when it comes to the convergence of the physical and digital worlds, it's even more important to remember to look for the human actor because they're the ones who primarily create the data layer that connects these worlds.

It's always been worth considering context in the design of experience. Content and interactions resonate best when they seem to flow naturally, which means considering where a user (or shopper or patient or person in some other role) might start, how they might continue, and what they will consider a successful finish.

It's even more important to consider context when it involves the physical reality of a person's surroundings, their device and bandwidth limitations, their environmental distractions, and more.

With or without connected devices, relating lived human experience to a virtual abstraction of that experience can lead the way to the discovery of meaningful patterns within human-generated data.

The Human Component of the Internet of Things

The buzz about the "Internet of Things" has been going on for a while. Fundamentally, it's about connecting devices to the internet and web, and to each other. It's any item that could/can use an internet connection.

The big deal is about the data it can/could send.

These devices potentially have a wide range of uses: for automation of various personal or business processes; for just-in-time reminders about purchasing supplies; for proactive maintenance; for intelligence insights into usage or related data with other devices.

Sixteen billion connected devices are forecasted to join the Internet of Things by the end of 2021, and by 2018 there will be more connected things than mobile devices according to Ericsson[13]. According to McKinsey, six types of applications are emerging in two broad categories: *information and analysis* and *automation and control.*[14]

Information and analysis includes tracking behavior, enhanced situational awareness, and sensor-driven decision analytics. *Automation and control* includes process optimization, optimized resource consumption, and complex autonomous systems.

Sometimes these devices are also called "smart" devices, but the only thing that makes many of them smart is that they have some data-enabled threshold for alerts, for modifying settings, or for responding to external stimuli in a specialized, programmatic way. For example, a normal, non-internet-connected thermostat can react to external stimuli like increasing room temperatures by also increasing the fan speed of the air-conditioning and cooling the room until it reaches a set temperature. A "smart" or internet-connected thermostat, though, will have that same ability but also may have the ability to: check local forecasts to see if the outside temperature is increasing or decreasing; determine from your settings how long it will be before you're home from work; or vary the energy expended to cool the room accordingly.

In other words, they're still "smart" in only a very limited way. They're more cleverly useful than they are smart.

(By the way we're awfully quick to call connected devices "smart," while at the same time our culture and media made intellectualism a challenging characteristic to display. What is the benefit to claiming "smart"-ness for our devices and not for ourselves?)

Here's the thing, though.

The term *Internet of Things* is at least partially misleading, since a great deal of the "things" only have relevance to human interaction and experience. Our movements and interactions generate data points, in a vast and expanding cosmos of data points, which only truly relate to each other in how they characterize and give dimension to the human experience. Otherwise, who cares? Who wants to know anything about what a smart refrigerator says about cooling patterns or its contents unless that information, in concert with a wearable fitness band, perhaps, paints a picture of the human life it services, and what that person chooses for nourishment?

In other words, it's still what it all *means* that matters. No raw data on its own is particularly interesting until a pattern emerges. Patterns indicate choices, actions, trends—human actors behaving in whatever way they behave. And we, the analysts, the sociologists, the marketers, the observers, are here to examine the data for those patterns, to ask the data what it will reveal about our fellow humans and their wants and needs and tendencies and fears and annoyances and habits.

Of course meaning is subjective, as it is in every case. And here is the difference between significance in a statistical sense and significance in a storytelling sense. Perhaps a data pattern emerges that points to a clear, unambiguous trend in human behavior. We can quantitatively observe this pattern, and *know* that this trend exists. But when we're exploring the qualitative side of the story, trying to deduce meaning from the trend, we potentially run into trouble. Because our own biases are likely to get involved in the narrative. Our own behaviors weave into the process.

Kids and data

There's also another consideration: kids.

In fact, parents often post information about their kids even before they're born, creating a data trail around them from moment one.

Internet-connected baby monitors, tracking systems at schools, and all sorts of other data-intensive devices and systems are creating the data-heavy framework kids are growing up into.

It's understandably nightmarish to think of privacy and security violations where children's devices are concerned. A couple discovered that a stranger had hacked into their baby monitor and was spying in on their three-year-old toddler, and even saying disturbing things to the child through the speaker.[15] The hacker used the night-vision lens to follow their movements in the room.

There are starting to be a lot of "smart" toys, and that's attaching data to kids' usage patterns long before they're old enough to post ill-considered selfies.

For businesses that market to parents and sell children's toys, clothing, and other stuff, targeting is tempting. But we need to tread extra carefully around this.

Kate O'Neill

The Data Trail: Everything Has Data History

I'm sitting in a hotel lobby working on this book, and conscious of the data layer, the digital experience layer all around me. People sitting in the lobby are on their phones and laptops, browsing and interacting on social media, checking in on Foursquare, checking flight times, ordering food to be delivered, making dinner reservations, buying odds and ends to be delivered to them back home, playing online games, texting with friends.

And all of it generates a data trail. All of it is trackable somewhere at some level, and much of it is traceable to this location. A good deal of it is happening on this hotel's Wi-Fi network.

Someone posts a photo to Instagram, and its location is tagged as the hotel. And maybe it has the hashtag "#nashville." Or maybe "#musiccity." All of the photos being posted today with those hashtags are connected at the joint of their metadata, and in a way, all of the people who posted and who will like those photos are therefore also connected by that metadata.

That's the most interesting part of it, isn't it? How we get connected to each other by the data we create. How we create an exoskeleton of bits around us through the location tags and geo-mapped transactions we engage in. How we live our lives a little more split every day between two worlds: the purely physical one around us, and the virtual/digital one that exists on screens and in the ether. We tap into our virtual world amid these fleeting moments of connectedness.

None of this is news to you, of course. You know we have FOMO and digital detoxes. You know the distraction of inboxes and notifications and likes and direct messages. You know the struggle to be present with your family and friends while your phone is lighting up with alerts.

It's not just the tension to live in these two worlds that makes this interesting, though; it's that we are the layer that connects the two worlds. There is no point to big data without humanity and human interaction and human experience. Sure, machines and systems produce mountains of data in their autonomous functioning, but their functioning is usually somehow in service of a human outcome. Manufacturing machines track their own production, but the point of their production is human

40

consumption, by and large.

***

Everything you see in the physical world surrounding you has a data history. I see coffee on shelves, and its production, from roasting to packaging, has had digital tracking components. It has a data trail.

Everything you see in the physical world surrounding you has a data history.

What makes this data trail interesting is not the coffee. It's the fact that the coffee is intended for human consumption. Everything is tracked not for the sake of tracking coffee, not for the love of data, but so that it is profitable for humans, purchasable by humans, and enjoyable for humans.

But even more so, we ourselves have a personal data trail, which we leave through our interactions with our phones, with cash registers, with security cameras, with sensors, with our cars and transit, and more. Or, as James Bamford put it in *Wired* when writing in 2012 about the National Security Agency's data center in Bluffdale, Utah, "parking receipts, travel itineraries, bookstore purchases, and other digital 'pocket litter[16]'."

There are, of course, huge privacy implications of that trail.

***

Increasingly, we spend our waking lives tethered to the digital devices that free us from the mundanity of being online only while seated at a desk. (And for that matter, many of us are connected while we sleep.) These devices by design collect and transmit data about us, logging our surroundings, our circumstances, and our behavior at various levels of abstraction: our kinesthetic data (think: apps that use an accelerometer), our biometric data (think: apps that track how many steps we take or how many flights of stairs we climb), our auditory environment (think: apps that collect a sample of music and identify a song), the frequency and timing of our interactions with the digitally connected world, and so on.

These devices are also connected to each other. And "Things" (as in "Internet of") that don't even register to us as "devices," such as cars and refrigerators, are increasingly tracking their own data around us; and that data potentially meshes with the data our carried devices are tracking. There's a staggering amount of it (data, that is), transmitting rapidly, silently, and invisibly, structurally describing our environment so that it can be parsed and understood, and opportunistically reshaped by analysts, technologists, and designers.

And that's only the passive stuff—the data tracked as a byproduct of using your iPhone or wearing your FitBit. We haven't even touched on the oceans of data we actively create with our Facebook pictures of Elf on the Shelf, our Spotify playlists, our inspirational quote tweets, our endless retro-filtered latte foam pictures on Instagram.

According to research compiled by the data analytics company Domo, in every minute of the day, there are four million Google searches, 204 million emails, over 2,460,000 Facebook posts, and over 277,000 tweets. Then there's the seventy-two hours of video uploaded to YouTube each minute, not to mention activity on Instagram, Tumblr, Flickr, Foursquare, and all the time and money spent shopping online. In fact those numbers are more than two years old, so you can bet they're now even higher.[17]

To these we add hashtags, links to friends, comments, hearts, likes, and favorites; and what potentially emerges, if we are to assemble the data just so, is a connect-the-dots picture of our projected selves. The Self on the Shelf, as it were.

Of course this raises questions about privacy. How do we ensure that our most personal and vulnerable information is kept from systems that could abuse it? It raises questions about security. What decisions do we make about the devices we use and the systems with which we choose to interact based on how safe we believe them to be? What determines private? What determines safe? What determines a reasonable trade-off for private and safe? Is it convenience? Is it cost? Do we make these decisions intentionally or without consideration?

It also raises questions about what it means to be human in the midst of all this digital infrastructure. Every moment of our online lives is immortalized in ever-expanding metadata.

What does it mean to be so well-documented? How does our long digital shadow affect the light we choose to shine on ourselves?

If we've created a connected consciousness by turning our devices into data paparazzi, we may need a moment to fix our collective hair. It's not idle talk when marketers say businesses need strategy for social media; it's because that kind of spotlight invites empty vamping for the camera. If you don't set your intentions in advance, you'll struggle to follow through, and your missteps will echo throughout dimensions of data and be etched in archives.

Part of the human experience is to be self-aware and socially aware. Self-awareness grows from recognizing when you don't live up to your intentions. Social awareness grows from understanding your impact on others. We have the means to measure, by some proxy, how we live up to our intentions, and how we impact others. The strategy we set today provides the framework for improvement tomorrow. You can measure almost anything; it's all being tracked. You just need to decide what's meaningful to pay attention to.

***

If we focus instead on the potential for delight, we can imagine how to design the experiences on behalf of corporations, organizations, institutions, and entities to maximize the richness of what the overlay of digital and physical can accomplish. We seek out where and how our digital selves transcend our physical limitations, where we have the limitlessness of global knowledge and resources at our fingertips and it adapts to our contextual needs, making our lives a little richer, a little less frustrating, a little more delightful, a little more satisfying. Or even sometimes a *lot* more delightful.

Our Digital Selves

Clearly digital culture has gone well beyond status updates. We've progressed beyond pictures of coffee and cats. From what a person posts, shares, likes, and clicks, you could form a pretty interesting sketch-level avatar of who they are: including the quotes, jokes, memes, news stories, feel-good viral videos, selfies, and rants. What they find funny, what they value, what news stories engage them, whom they want to impress, what kind of content makes them linger long enough to read an article or watch a video all the way through.

Fear of Missing Out Versus Fear of Not Sharing

Pundits in the past few years have written a lot about FOMO, or the "fear of missing out," which is the sense of anxiety that if you're offline or not following your social feeds, you're missing out on what everyone else might be sharing. But I think there's a correlating anxiety that's less discussed: about missing out on sharing what you experience. Fear of Not Sharing, or something like that. Because more and more, I get the sense that our experiences don't feel real or valid to us until we've shared them with our followers and gotten a few likes on them. Preferably a whole lot of likes, and a few re-shares.

* * *

I took this photo in June 2016 of tourists posing for pictures on the pedestals at the Louvre museum in Paris. Were you really at the Louvre if you didn't take a selfie in front of the pyramid?

It may seem like vanity or insecurity that drives us to do this, but I suspect it's more nuanced than that. I suspect it's because we actually live our online lives in ways we don't fully understand yet and can't yet articulate well. We create an aspirational avatar of our selves with every bit of content we share.

We create an aspirational avatar of our selves

with every bit of content we share.

Our Digital Selves Are Our Aspirational Selves

Years ago, I took on a project at Magazines.com to understand what a forward-looking brand promise could be for an online aggregator of print magazine subscriptions. What it led to was an understanding that people have a different relationship to magazines than they have to other media they consume, and that their magazine subscriptions, taken as a set, represent an aspirational view of themselves. People who may never play guitar on stage subscribe to *Performer Magazine*, and there is no requirement for a tidy home before subscribing to *Better Homes and Gardens*. (In fact, the word *better* in that magazine's title is a real clue, isn't it?)

While that may not seem like an earth-shattering insight, it was indeed a focusing one for a company that wasn't really sure what it would have to offer its customers in an increasingly digital-content-oriented future.

In the meantime, even more than we knew at the time, social media and everything else has given the content we consume a hard shake, like a snow globe dispersing tiny glittering flecks of content everywhere. Now our aspirational selves can be understood in dramatically greater detail by analyzing the patterns of the shiny content flecks that capture our attention for brief moments in fleeting ways every day online.

Because of that, our digital selves now more fully represent our most aspirational selves in a far more nuanced way than any of our traditional offline media or brand affinities have ever done. Our digital selves contain so much inherent information about what moves us to act and what we feel compelled to say and with whom we seek to connect. They are a composite of what we search for and what we ultimately buy. They contain a map of what we think is important enough and aligned enough with who we feel we are in that moment to share with our friends. Also included in our digital selves is our medical history, our academic record, our late-night searches for old lovers, our location-tagged vacation photographs. In an aggregate sense, they are truly the abstractions of everything we want, everything we love, everything we say we need—and yet often what we habitually do in spite of all that.

Yet as we engage online, we keep getting admonished to put down our phones and join the "real world." But our virtual presence is real to us, too, and the interactions we have with other people online are often dimensionally more connected to our aspirational selves than the ones we are able to have in person. If you're a teenager surrounded by your family—whom you did not choose to be with—but you can interact virtually with people who genuinely share an interest of yours, it can be difficult to pull yourself from that virtual realm and focus on the people and the world around you.

The data that connects the people and those moments is all out there, being mined for insights every day by a wide variety of entities. The motive is profit, generally speaking, but if our digital selves are really who we aspire to be, we are also duty bound to show our digital selves respect.

> If our digital selves are really who we aspire to be, we are also duty bound to show our digital selves respect.

On the other hand, maybe some of that content is just sparkly fake snow. For all the admonitions to be "authentic" online, we don't yet have a useful framework for understanding how weaving elements of fakeness into our virtual identities—carefully staging Instagram photos, posting lighthearted status updates while we're bored and depressed at home—might play into our aspirational understanding of ourselves. Which person are you, really: the one you've always been, or the one you're someday hoping to be?

And Beyond: Virtual Identities

If our digital selves represent our aspirational selves, then who are we when we adopt virtual identities? Do we create the self we wish we were, the self we wish others could see, the self best suited to the game or the context, or some other version of self? Like digital selves, virtual selves are often experimental selves: the versions of our identities we'd like to try on, to see what fits.

But in as much as our digital selves are our aspirational selves, our physical selves are the more sensory and sensual selves. And senses play into meaning. Part of acknowledging the importance of place—physical place—is a form of showing respect to our physical selves, too.

Until virtual experiences can engage our physical forms and senses as fully as purely physical experiences do, they'll need to be supplemented with physical experiences. And since physical experiences can rarely engage our minds and imagination as fully as purely digital experiences, they benefit from supplementation with digital experiences, too.

Ultimately, the convergence of physical and digital experiences, if we do it right, can be the pinnacle of meaningful experience, engaging our senses, engaging our bodies, engaging our minds, and engaging our projected, aspirational selves.

Beyond Personal Brand

All of this is why the popular notion of "personal brand" is so stilted, artificial, and even arbitrary. Yes, we do have the opportunity to be intentional about the self we reinforce. But human beings are not businesses with a singular focus and mission; we grow, our identities are fluid, and eventually, if we're lucky to survive long enough to become a little enlightened, we evolve. Our old aspirational selves are no longer aspirational then; they're our past aspirational selves, the empty shells of who we once wanted to be. But like empty shells sometimes do, they may provide useful temporary housing for some other being that comes along after us, sharing our old content as their own revelation.

Meanwhile, we move forward, creating new dimensions of our selves with every interaction, dragging our digital detritus behind us.

Bearing all this in mind, in our roles as creators and designers of the experiences that adapt to the contours of others' digital selves, we have an exciting opportunity and a great responsibility. We get to dream up interactions that more fully integrate our fellow humans' physical surroundings and beings with their digital selves and lives, just as other creators and designers are shaping the experiences we will encounter. It's easy to think of "big data" or even your own customer data in an abstract way, and develop interactions that manipulate or exploit the vulnerability of the people whose data you have access to. But remembering that the data is someone's digital self, just as your data is your digital self, may encourage us to have a little healthy respect for the power and identity of that data. Since each of us is increasingly vulnerable to the whims of algorithmic influence, once again, the Golden Rule—do unto others as you would have them do unto you—has a powerful place in respectful data-guided marketing and experience design.

People, Community, and Connection to Place

If people and their data are the connective layer between the physical world and the digital world, then it also stands to reason that community is yet another dimension of that connectivity. Community develops offline in relation to places all the time: in neighborhoods, churches, workplaces, and so on. But even in those places the communities aren't just about the places: they're also about shared ideas and identity even in subgroups. The online versions of community often take similar shapes: around a place, like a social platform, but clustered around subcultural identities.

It's also interesting how technologies that purport in some way to bridge the physical and digital worlds bring people together or don't. Think of Foursquare, and what at least initially was the promise of using Foursquare check-ins. It seemed that it could have been a seamless log of our movements, the places we have seen and visited and experienced, a way to connect with friends who are in our path, and a serendipity engine for meeting new people along the way.

I even had that kind of scenario play out once. I'm notorious among my friends as an early-to-bed, early-to-rise person, but one night when I lived in Nashville I had visitors and I was showing them the honky-tonks on Broadway (as you do) when I checked in to one of them on Foursquare. Two of my friends saw me check into a bar at the unlikely hour of eleven p.m. on a weeknight, and they surprised me by showing up. It was spontaneous and fun, and I got to introduce them to my out-of-town friends. The whole experience was better and more delightful because of my ability to make my whereabouts incidentally visible to my friends and their ability to see it and act on it. (My real friends, mind you. Had these been more casual acquaintances, their sudden appearance might have been awkward. But it wasn't, and it need not be.)

What is available in that opportunity?

If we want to borrow from the check-in model, we'd have to ask users to trade off some measures of privacy to make the most of this opportunity, but that can be done in levels. As a user, I may want to select layers of friends who can have visibility into my every move versus those who only see what I choose to share in review, versus the strangers who have chosen to allow some of their identity to be accessible because we're in the same place. There are security measures to be taken here, but the opportunities are rich.

In general, as we design for integrated experiences, it helps to be aware that the nature of community online, as offline, leans heavily on association with place, and the experience of connection within it.

Some online experiences rely almost completely on how a community of users relates to some notion of place. Yelp without customer reviews would just be a searchable Yellow Pages (and a search feature does add value, but not nearly as much as wisdom-of-crowds[18] reviews do).

And yet most of what we experience online, we still experience while we are physically alone. Could it be that our online selves are connecting in community in ways we don't yet have a framework and vocabulary for? The dynamics of community as they play out online are still forming and evolving.

Yet digital culture is an observable phenomenon—different online spaces clearly have different cultures.

As we sit alone in front of our computers, or detach from our physical companions to interact with our phones, we are connecting with virtual communities online and shaping those spaces.

While human beings are physical and finite, our virtual selves are contextual essences, mixed and remixed in endless combinations.

Selfies and Metadata Dimensionality

Every time I visit the Cloud Gate sculpture in Chicago (known affectionately as "The Bean"), I can't help but notice that everyone is taking selfies. A great many of them are posted to Instagram and tagged with the location of the sculpture, but across several different tags and hashtags. Some of the variations may be unavoidable, and it may even add to the delight of the place that someone gets to choose whether they call it "Cloud Gate" or "The Bean." But it also decouples the experiences for those two sets of visitors who choose differently. The variation makes it more difficult to analyze place data, whenever that is a meaningful task.

Cloud Gate in Chicago, also known as "The Bean"

Here's an opportunity: If you are responsible for the place, you can combine the colloquial name for the place with the given name for the place. You can post it somewhere visible for people to use, and they can connect through time with other people who have shared their experience.

I gave a talk on "The Meaning of Place" and was asked about how to create meaning for a place with social media. One suggestion I had was to embrace the noteworthiness of a place and make it easy for visitors to feel they were participating in the place's legacy. They can't do that if they can't find the right location or if it doesn't occur to them to use a certain hashtag, so you can make it easy by posting signs. It could be of value, if permission is granted or implied, to pop up a notice on someone's phone or device to let them know they're in a particular place of significance, and allow them to be part of the culture and community that have participated in its legacy. Some platforms and tools have features that function like this in limited ways: Yelp and Foursquare both send push notifications about nearby restaurants and other venues of interest, and Instagram places and Snapchat geo-filters both connect a person dimensionally with other people who have visited or participated in a place or place-centric event. That kind of push interaction is, of course, rife with privacy concerns and contrary user preferences, so the easiest way to promote that continuity is to use the physical surroundings to connect the visitors digitally.

CHAPTER FIVE

The Meaning of Place

What is the meaning of *place*? In examining what we mean when we talk about place, we can deconstruct and reconstruct that understanding to be useful in dealing with digital experiences. There's a difference between knowing what *place* generally means and knowing what *a place* means, or what makes a place meaningful. Let's examine that, too.

What is "Place"? What Does Any Place Mean?

What is place? What does place mean? What does a given place mean?
   What is the meaning of place? What makes a place meaningful?
   What does our understanding of place do for us?
   All of these questions yield potentially different answers.
   Let's start with what place is. Obviously we tend think of place as our physical surroundings, but given our framework here, we'll just say "surroundings" so that we can eventually include digital experiences. Part of what defines place for us is an identity relative to our experience of it, and a relative sense of how other people do or don't affect the experience, whether through a sense of community or privacy. I don't expect a sense of community in my backyard, for example, but perhaps part of what defines that space for me is that I do sense privacy when I'm there. Part of what defines that place is the relationship it has to people: as in, that there generally are none, unless I invite them.
   When we talk about meaning, we are looking for significance,

connectivity. In thinking about what place means, we are looking for clues about what a place conveys into context, what signifiers it brings with it. The important thing about place is that it grounds our physical surroundings, and links us to those around us in that space. For a moment, at least, we share some dimension of cultural identity, and an experience of our sense of surroundings.

The "place" in question could be a store, a hospital, a public park, an airport, a museum, a corporate office, a zoo, or even a city or state or country. Really just about anything. In any case, someone is invested in the development of the idea of that place, whether they think about it that way or not. It is important to cultivate the brand experience of that place, and understand what makes it recognizably different from another space that shares superficial or functional characteristics.

Placemaking and the Idea of Intentional Place

Some places are designed *very* intentionally—such as a movie set—because the design relates directly to the success of the endeavor. Retail environment design is somewhat like this, where every element is considered as to how it encourages buying behavior, although not *merely* buying behavior, but merchandised product that is most profitable or somehow most relevant to sell.

Hospitals and healthcare facilities are designed to promote hygiene, sterility, and trust as well as the *ideas* of hygiene, sterility, and trust.

Other types of places that are often planned, designed, or nurtured very carefully for a particular kind of outcome occur within the fields of architecture, landscape design, interior design, museums, libraries, and more. We could also think about conceptual "spaces" like radio, media, and other esoteric non-space places.

But of course also in digital. In user experience, information architecture, customer experience, brand strategy, and marketing, the context of the digital "surroundings," in a sense, are critical to understand for influence, behavior strategy, and more

So can we map one to the other? Should we? What do we learn by holding up physical placemaking ideas to digital, and what do we learn by examining the developing disciplines of digital strategy and placemaking for cues about how our built environment should be designed to be more effective, more pleasing, more meaningful.

A model that is valuable to study is placemaking. What is placemaking? It's an approach to planning that prioritizes the relevance of the space to the community, in a sense.

Placemaking as a term has been around in niche discussions of urban planning for decades, but it seems to be everywhere right now, principally because people across a variety of industries and disciplines have started to recognize the benefits of the intentional design of a place-centric experience. The way placemaking is described and approached seems to vary from source to source, but in general, from its origins with luminaries like Jane Jacobs and William H. Whyte[19] to its current usages, it tends to be about facilitating an integrative, inclusive, meaningful use of a space. The space in question could be as focused as a retail environment display or as broad as an entire city. The various ways people naturally use the space and how the space *could* be used are both major considerations in design and redesign.

Many of the elements we've discussed for Integrative Human Experience Design are also attributes of placemaking: context-specific, visionary, adaptable[20], etc.

In some communities, a placemaking approach might surface a need for green space, or a community park. Or a community garden. Placemaking would mean a very intentional effort to create that needed space on the premise that it will benefit the community.

Placemaking isn't the right model for every integrated experience challenge, but it lends us a great deal of insight about the development of meaningful experiences in place.

If you look at someone like the Danish architect Jan Gehl, whose work is around human life in cities, there are plenty of parallels to digital experience. As Gehl et al. assert in their 2006 book *New City Life*, contemporary urban planning is totally different from what it was before, say, World War II.

Now—with the proliferation of the private auto, suburban shopping malls, numerous home entertainment offerings, spacious backyards and many other incentives for us to simply stay at home—people venture out in public because they want to rather than because they have to.[21]

* * *

55

In a similar fashion, we can observe what makes people want to interact in physical space when they don't have to. What brings someone to a store when they could buy online? What brings someone to a restaurant when they could have food delivered?

What Is Digital Placemaking? (Or Human Experience Design?)

The work of digital experience design, then, is to create a meaningful sense of place that serves people and/or community. It might serve a business purpose, and that's okay, but it has to have some authentic relevance.

Cities evolve through history and layers of culture, but that doesn't mean that city planners don't have a role in proactively developing infrastructure, utilities, and resources to make the quality of life in the city better. You can find a capitalist motive there, too: A well-planned city is not only a better place to live, but also it offers more economic stability and a more assured tax base.

An online space—for example, an e-commerce website—may not seem like a reasonable parallel because it's a brand-owned space with an explicitly commercial function. But retailers—at least, savvy retailers—pay attention to the implicitly expressed interests of their visitors, those who buy as well as those who don't, through website analytics.

Designers talk about the analogy of "cowpaths" to explain the idea that cows, or people for that matter, won't necessarily follow the predicted path if they find that it doesn't lead to water. They'll carve out their own, and that trail will be visible to anyone following them. It reveals what they want and how they went about getting it.

Humans aren't cattle, but we, too, carve out our own paths when what we want isn't readily presented to us. If you're in charge of the website where a steady trail of people enters on a particular product page, uses the site search function to try to find another product, and then leaves, you have yourself something to investigate and improve.

Creating a sense of place in a digital experience is about the fundamentals of satisfying visitors' needs, but it's also about recognizing and creating a sense of identity that's shared among the visitors.

Starbucks, "Third Place," and the Power of Strategic Framing

In the early 1980s, Howard Schultz was visiting Italy and became captivated by the spirit of the Italian coffeehouses. He loved how the Italians seemed to be living balanced lives, and he loved the idea of a "Third Place," where people could go to create community: a place that was not home and not work.

So Starbucks isn't about coffee; it's about "Third Place." Netflix isn't about movies; it's about options for escape. IKEA isn't about furniture; it's about self-empowered style. Southwest Airlines isn't about cheap airfare; it's about bringing the customer into the decision to embrace operational efficiencies. (Think: peanuts, humor, etc.) Apple isn't about computers or phones; it's about design.

It is quite likely that a great deal of the reason Starbucks succeeds is because of this philosophy at the heart of the business strategy. Schultz had not only a product to sell, but also an experience—and a nuanced one at that. Strategy that reaches well beyond planning and examines purpose and metaphor is more likely to be transformative.

Brands need an understanding of what they're about. Strategic meaning. Strategic purpose.

It's similar to but not necessarily the "why" Simon Sinek talks about— not always the mission, but more about a crystallizing idea.

Having an understanding of your strategic purpose/strategic meaning allows you to move confidently through decisions, focus on what matters, and develop much more meaningful relationships with your customers. From there, you can develop more meaningful marketing, more relevant tech trends, and more aligned operations; and all the facets of the business can more readily fall into place around the idea.

Moreover, the chances are better with a strategic metaphor framework that you'll hit all the resonant notes. You can develop a strategy that helps you succeed while respecting the human beings you're doing business with. When your purpose relates to how people assign meaning to the places they go, as is the case with Starbucks, it's even more important to be clear and intentional with that framing.

Stories and Place

I often work at coffee shops. A lot of other people do, too, of course. But since it's my nature to think about what makes different human experiences meaningful in different ways, I sometimes find myself deconstructing the experience of working in a coffee shop. I'm looking for what we can learn about designing experiences, both online and offline.

The opening question is: *"Why?"* What is the value of working on my smallish laptop screen on a hard chair at a crowded coffee shop as opposed to sitting at my desk in my apartment, where I have a big display for docking my laptop, access to a huge supply of teas, and slippers to make myself as comfortable as I like? What would make me choose to pay and be inconvenienced for discomfort and fewer amenities?

You could propose "because there are no distractions," and yes, for some people (including myself), that's probably a part of it. After all, if you live with cats, you know they can be pretty insistent about getting attention. I can only imagine how insistent kids might be. But then again, you're adding a whole lot of distractions when you work in a coffee shop, or another "Third Place." You're adding a whole lot of people to have to tune out and ignore.

But ignore them you can. In general you're likely to perceive less of a sense of obligation to acknowledge and respond to the distractions you encounter in a coffee shop than you would, say, at the office, when your colleague shows up at your desk asking for that TPS report. Beyond that, I don't have to think about the small stack of paperwork on my desk. At the coffee shop, I've effectively eliminated it from my context and can concentrate on the work I've come to do.

Also, you're trading familiar distractions for more interesting distractions, and perhaps more stimulating distractions, in a sense. For someone who thrives on creative inspiration, that can make a tremendous difference, whether tackling creative or mundane tasks.

The next question that occurs to me is: *"When?"* How often is it productive and beneficial to work in a Third Place versus the usual place? What's the ideal combination of familiar and new to inspire but not distract?

For example, I find that I do really powerful brainstorming and big, think-y, strategic work in airplanes. I always assume there's a combination of factors in play: turning off internet connectivity, probably first and foremost, but also being in a constrained environment where it is literally a challenge to get up from the seat and do anything other than focus on the space right in front of me. Those factors seem to come together to reward me with some of the clearest thinking work I ever do. But then I wonder: Would I be able to rely on having such breakthrough thinking if I increased my frequency of travel? Maybe it's the pacing of it that works. I travel far more than the average person, but not as much as many frequent business travelers do, and perhaps the relatively limited availability of the airplane context keeps it fresh. I'm looking to experiment with that a bit over the next year or two.

And in the process of writing this book, I found it helpful sometimes to take my laptop to bookstores with cafés, where I could write surrounded by the context of selling books. I don't know if it really helped me on a subconscious level to power through and finish, but I always paid attention on my way in and my way out, browsing the new nonfiction table, thinking about what I was working on in that context.

In any case, asking "when" in relation to changing the context of place is important in designing optimally meaningful experiences. At a certain level, it's the heart of what work-life balance is about.

You're probably already ahead of me on thinking through the next questions: *"where," "what," "how,"* and *"who."*

Well, the *"where"* question is already all about place, so we're fundamentally examining it already. But to frame it up in a way we can apply to designing experiences, the place you're in is a significant part of the context of your interactions. Place creates opportunities for stories and interactions.

In your *home*, the opportunity for interactions is limited to a small and mostly repeating set. But home is where, in some respects, you probably have the most control over your environment and experiences.

In your *office* or fixed workplace, the opportunity for interactions is limited to a small and mostly repeating set. Depending on your position, you probably have some degree of control over your environment and experiences.

In a *Third Place*, though—such as a coffee shop, a bar, an airport, or a park—the opportunities are pretty much unlimited and the opportunity for novelty is much higher. Although you have little control within the place itself, you have in some ways the most important kind of control: You get to choose to be in this place ("where") for however long ("when") for whatever purpose ("what and why") and how much you acknowledge your surroundings ("who").

It's not that one is inherently better than the others; sometimes the interactions and novelty introduce *too much* distraction and annoyance. Today, for example, an uncommonly beautiful woman was seated to my right at the window bench, and for a while (until I put headphones on and drowned it out) I was privy to overhearing her being hit on by strange men. Some were one-and-done approaches; one in particular was a prolonged attempt to wear her down and get her interest. She was unfailingly polite, but I thought (and tweeted) if this is as tedious as it is for me, I can't imagine how tedious it must be for her.

I digress. But that digression is more or less the point. In a coffee shop or other Third Place, you're placed in proximity of these kinds of micro-happenings that don't really add up to much and don't really change your life; but taken as a whole, they add color and perspective and dimension to our lives. It's an opportunity for empathy and framing up your perspective alongside countless other people you can observe.

What Else?

On top of that, if you start imagining, as I do, the data being generated all around me by everyone interacting and transacting with digital outlets—like the cash register, their phones, their laptops, their wearable fitness trackers, my tweets about the guys hitting on the woman, and so on—it is a truly fascinating picture of the layers of place.

What does this tell us about designing places? About designing experiences?

As we look at how and where people choose to spend their time online, we can see the influence of place on meaningful experiences: People engage frequently with Facebook partly because it is a place you go to have a Third Place kind of experience. There are distractions, but not too many. The context of Twitter is particularly free of obligations: There is no expectation that anyone can keep up with the volume of content generated there, so you can wade into it like a stream and wade back out without having to acknowledge anyone or anything.

Where things get really interesting is in communities like Meetup.com and Nextdoor.com, where inherently and by design there is an overlap between offline relationships and online interactions. We can ignore etiquette to some extent when we're dealing with online abstractions we're not even sure are real people; but when your neighbor is ranting about guns or that new bar down the street, it becomes uncomfortably close and hard to ignore.

How Do Online "Places" and "Spaces" Create Meaning?

A place creates meaning through the associations it has, through the culture it fosters, through the community it creates, through the identity it retains. Culture is defined variously as the arts, knowledge, beliefs, customs, humanities, and other intellectual achievements of a collective people. In essence, it is about shared ideas. Perhaps the embodiment of shared ideas. Communities themselves sometimes have a culture. The meaning of a place has to do with its identity. Identity is how an individual crystallizes the reactions to the social and cultural environment around them.

Online places and spaces can do this just as offline places can.

If you don't think so, look at the cultural dynamics of Instagram versus Tumblr, or Twitter versus Facebook. Or Snapchat versus any of them. There are intricacies to the way social norms have evolved in each platform, visual vocabularies that have taken hold in each space. Twitter, for example, has fostered an environment of media junkies, social justice activists, and one-line comedians, in addition to inspirational quotes, selfies, and the rest of the stream. (Well, and a lot of harassment, too. Let's not forget.) This same mix of dynamics doesn't exist in the same proportions in any other medium. It's a culture all its own, a place-specific microculture.

CHAPTER SIX

People in Place: Neighborhoods and Community

Many products and services are built around not just one person interacting at a time, but rather several or many people, in groups or en masse, in contact with each other or disjointed from each other's experiences. There are many variations, from Meetup to Second Life. As soon as you begin to think about the dynamics of planning for more than one person in relation to online spaces, virtual reality experiences, or any kind of group interaction, it starts to bring up questions about community.

Community is a hot topic in online marketing because the term has been adopted to mean the nurturing of a group of users of a product or service. But if you trace the idea of community back to offline, there are wonderful insights to be drawn from how community manifests in physical place. There are related concepts, such as neighborhoods, that may provide meaningful ideas to use in developing the next phase of multiperson interactions.

People trying to build coalitions in neighborhoods need the tried-and-true but slow and time-intensive method of going door to door for building community in the offline sense. The dynamics of community are like that: top-down community gets pushback; whereas bottom-up community takes patience and effort. But online, that model of approaching people one-by-one doesn't often translate. What would it mean to try to build community in a one-to-one sense using online tools?

So here we'll step back and examine what community is and what neighborhoods are, and see if we glean something valuable in the process.

What Community Is, Offline and Online

What does community mean for, say, a college campus? What are the dynamics that affect the way people relate to each other?

To some extent, it has to do with the aesthetics of a place—about the identity the people there share, as well as the shared culture.

What does community mean for a city like, say, Nashville? Or New York City? Or Omaha?

There are many ways to think about the meaning of a place, such as its identity, and the experiences one associates with it. But the one I think has the most profound sense of truth to me is that part of the meaning of any given place is in the community we create there.

By "there," I mean not only a place, but also the context of a place—such as a moment in time, and the people who were part of your community then. Like "school."

It's about connecting with the people who can own that experience, who will connect with the community there. Because community is meaning writ large.

Community is meaning writ large.

Neighborhood Memory

A refreshingly human take on pixels and place is the project undertaken by 596 Acres, a public land advocacy group in New York City that taps into the wonderful concept of "neighborhood memory" that's critical to understanding community and culture of a place. Through signs posted on vacant lots, a phone number, and a website, 596 Acres is tracking the stories and knowledge of people who've lived in a neighborhood and capturing them in digital form. But the integration of offline—meaning, in this case, local human interaction—and online is key:

> "'You can't make it all work with a website. You might need a website to understand the situation so you can help the people that live in

your city to solve problems,' Segal says. 'But without a local advocacy organization the thing doesn't work.'"[22]

There is a wonderful insight about place and community in how neighborhoods "remember" their culture through storytelling and cultural artifacts. In this case, digital tools will help to preserve the sense of a place. In some online communities, a sense of place, of sorts, needs to be designed intentionally to add significance to digital tools.

And consider sharing economy / experience economy brands like Airbnb, Uber, Lyft—multisided marketplaces around physical experiences that by definition need to design at some level both for community and for cross-channel, connected consumption. Place is inherent in the location-specific nature of the service; what they need to foster is their sense of significance in the community of that place.

Protecting Community Members

One of the elements of fostering community surely comes down to safety: how safe you're making the community members feel about being in the space, whether it's a physical space or a digital one. When we think about online platforms like Twitter or Facebook, we may find valuable lessons in the attempts to reclaim safe place by community.

Safety and Online Community: Twitter and #GamerGate

In an integrated approach to experience design for any placemaking or digital strategy, the dynamics of how the interactions will play out need to be thought through. Will marginalization occur as a result of anonymity? How can that be counterbalanced?

In the case of Twitter—a format that encourages quick, brief thoughts and lends itself to anonymity—major controversies have arisen around tensions between users or groups of users and their detractors and harassers. The #GamerGate debacle was one such spiraling meltdown involving the gaming industry that resulted in death threats and other harassment, most notably toward women. Twitter also indexes high for usage among African Americans, and as a result, a culture known as

#BlackTwitter has emerged; but outspoken members of this group are often targets of harassment as well. As a result of these and other issues, Twitter is constantly being criticized by some of its most prominent users for not doing enough to protect its community.

In December 2015, Twitter announced that it had hired Jeffrey Siminoff, who had previously headed up diversity at Apple, to be their vice president of diversity and inclusion. On the surface that sounds positive, but the fact that he's a white man drew fire from some on Twitter, predominantly women and people of color who felt that hiring a white man for the role showed a lack of nuanced understanding on Twitter's part about what the real issues were.

The agility with which accounts can be created on Twitter has been an asset to many people in developing projects and corresponding accounts with a niche focus. People regularly create accounts to tweet on behalf of a dog or to automate tweets from a bot.

But those same interaction mechanics—of being able to spring up numerous accounts as sock puppets and spew hateful rhetoric at a person until they block those accounts—may have led some members of the Twitter community to become targets.

CHAPTER SEVEN

The Ethics of Connected Experiences

In many ways, we've become the frog in the pot of water, ignoring the rising temperature of the hot water we're in. The services many of us enjoy using every day ask to track our activity or examine our conversations.

As the saying goes, if you're not paying for the product, you *are* the product.

Because the data involved in connected experiences also includes our physical location, that means we're vulnerable in physical ways. For example, in the days after the launch of the incredibly popular augmented reality game *Pokémon GO* launched, at least one incident occurred where muggers used the game to lure players to a location in order to rob at least one player.

Does that mean we shouldn't experiment with integrated experiences? Not at all. We simply must do so with an awareness of the very real impact our decisions may have on the people who interact with us.

Fair Isn't Always Fair

Imagine walking up to an airplane ticket counter, buying a ticket to Chicago, and being charged $359. Then, as you start to walk away from the counter, you hear the next person ask for a ticket to Chicago and be charged $279. Suppose you go back to the counter and ask the ticket agent why you had to pay more than the other customer, and suppose the agent tells you it is because you are wearing blue and the other person is wearing red—which is the airline's preferred color.

It's an absurd cxamplc, but only in particulars. In fundamentals, it's not unlike a lot of the disparity that happens in pricing all the time. Some of that disparity has to do with algorithms that have been encoded with certain biases, whether intentionally or unintentionally (see also the section on "Chapter Ten - Algorithms and AI"), while some of it is overzealous analysis and optimization efforts run amok.

Staples and prices based on proximity to competitors

A 2012 *Wall Street Journal* article and investigation showed that Staples was serving different prices to different users, and it seemed to have to do with location. More to the point, it seemed to be based on proximity to a competitor's store. If you were closer to a rival store when you pulled up the Staples website, you were more likely to see a discounted price. According to the article:

> Offering different prices to different people is legal, with a few exceptions for race-based discrimination and other sensitive situations. Several companies pointed out that their online price-tweaking simply mirrors the real world. Regular shops routinely adjust their prices to account for local demand, competition, store location and so on. Nobody is surprised if, say, a gallon of gas is cheaper at the same chain, one town over.
> But price-changing online isn't popular among shoppers. Some 76% of American adults have said it would bother them to find out that other people paid a lower price for the same product, according to the Annenberg Public Policy Center at the University of Pennsylvania.[23]

In fact marketers often experiment with revenue elasticity testing. For past employers and clients, I've been part of running quite a few A/B experiments on price with the aim of determining what price point seems to be most effective for making the most sales. It takes some calibration to get the price point right for a new offering. Should this widget be $12.99 or $15? Okay, more people are buying at the $12.99 price point, but is it because of the lower cost or the $.99 format of the numbers in the price? Let's try it at $12.99 and $11 to be sure. Okay, more people are still taking the $12.99 price, so we can either stop there and run with that price or run a few more tests to see if $11.99, $12.99, or $13.99 works best. You get the idea.

But what this means is that some companies are taking those results and saying, "People who came in on Macintosh computers keep buying at the higher price points, so let's identify them when they visit the website and push them a higher-priced offer since they're more likely to take it." Pushing out different pricing to different segments of customers? That's crossing an ethical line.

Fandango's exceptionally high ratings

Not all of the weirdness has to do with pricing, either. Online ratings have a tendency to skew toward the high side of the distribution anyway, but movie ratings on Fandango.com, provided by website users, tended to skew *very* high.

The data analysis website FiveThirtyEight explored the topic in 2015, pointing out the oddities in the presentation of ratings. User ratings were always being rounded up, rather than rounded off, resulting in an overall exaggerated average rating. They also noted that Fandango has a sales motive in selling movie tickets to consumers.

> Several sites have built popular rating systems: Rotten Tomatoes, Metacritic and IMDb each have their own way of aggregating film reviews. And while the sites have different criteria for picking and combining reviews, they have all built systems with similar values: They use the full continuum of their ratings scale, try to maintain consistency, and attempt to limit deliberate interference in their ratings.
>
> These rating systems aren't perfect, but they're sound enough to be useful.
>
> All that cannot be said of Fandango, a NBCUniversal subsidiary that uses a five-star rating system in which almost no movie gets fewer than three stars, according to a FiveThirtyEight analysis. [24]

Overly high ratings may not have as direct an impact on people as skewing prices on what seem like arbitrary factors (such as what kind of computer you use), but the overall takeaway here is that the use of data to drive experience comes with a certain amount of risk. As designers of experiences, we need to be responsible for not only the data we collect and use but also for responsibly collecting and using that data. In other words, we need to protect consumer privacy, and we also need to monitor the methods by which we use consumer data to target experiences so that they don't cross over the line of what's ethical and fair.

Moreover, as we consider the implications of this kind of inequity for connected experiences, it becomes clear that companies can use additional data sets and hardware like beacons to target us all based on things like our location data—and that starts to get even more dicey. So when we are the ones instigating that targeting through integrated experiences, we must be mindful of whether we've gone beyond offering relevance and into offering disproportionate opportunity on arbitrary factors.

The Ethical Burden of Too Much Data

Our objective in tracking data should be quite simple: because we can use it responsibly to align our brand purpose and objectives with our customers' or users' motivations and needs, and to gauge our effectiveness. Our data stores become more needlessly complex and ethically burdensome when we collect too much data we have no application for, or that the use of can in no way benefit the end user.

If our data collection exceeds that function, we increase our risks: the risks of exposure to breaches, and the risks of misguidedly using consumer data in a way that can only be regarded as manipulative, greedy, or simply untrustworthy.

The Ethical Burden of Data Collection

For example, an article in the *Independent* reports that Uber collects battery level information from users calling for rides. As a result, they know when your phone is about to die.[25] They also know that you're more likely to pay "surge" fares as a result. Now in this article, the company representative is very quick to say that they are not using the data; but nonetheless, that's a lot of what we might call "ethical burden" due to collecting data that doesn't readily align their motives and their customers' motives. If they're *going* to collect it, they should be looking for how its interpretation *can* align their motives with customers' motives—for example, developing a means of processing the ride in the background or expediting the response to a call.

Either of those objectives for collecting the data, if understood by customers, would foster delight, ultimately resulting in greater customer loyalty and word-of-mouth recommendations, which could lower their cost of new customer acquisition. When the company instead evaluates whether they could get away with surge charges in that scenario, they misalign: They only stand to benefit themselves and alienate customers. Even if they don't use the data, it has already become ethically burdensome.

So, does Uber deserve to have access to that data? Do any of our projects deserve the access we have? What are we doing to safeguard ourselves?

Access to user data is certainly now critical to contemporary marketing. The success of the user experience and the ability to improve it over time relies on the underpinnings of the data model, and how thoughtfully and intentionally it is created.

After all, another way to look at these developments is depth of data. Not too long ago, if you wanted to make informed online marketing decisions, you were happy to be working off of search data. All you had was words. Well, words, plus clicks. But mostly words.

Here's an example. If someone was searching for the phrase "common songs," they'd have to disambiguate between multiple interpretations of that query. It's most probable that they wanted to find songs by the artist Common. But they also could have meant songs that are commonly known, songs that everyone could sing along to—such as "Happy Birthday" or "This Land Is Your Land" or others.

As time has gone on, the data available to decode those types of ambiguities grew more sophisticated anyway: Beyond search terms and clicks, there were website visit histories, social graphs, social statuses, and more. Software built to offer ads and content to website visitors has gotten more sophisticated in its ability to infer what might be successful. Marketers don't necessarily have access to the breadth of this data up front, but they can design campaigns around conditional use of these characteristics.

Now with all this place-related data, you have movement, locations, and time to consider. If you're a marketer and you want to successfully make relevant and timely offers, you have to anticipate the place-related data. Anticipating it requires having enough empathy to hypothesize what might be happening as a person encounters triggers that make them want to buy or research a solution like yours. You have to be able to think about their context—their surroundings, their possible setup and equipment at the moment, their emotional state—as well as their outward indications, such as search terms, click path, and so on. And you have their location, which may or may not tell you anything directly; people may be doing their banking from within a retail store, their shopping on a sailboat, their news reading on the bus, or anything else.

So if we're going to be intentional about this convergence, we need to look at the different metaphors we use to talk about and represent our physical and digital worlds. We can examine what associations we're making with different experiences, and how we actually experience them.

Is There an Ethical Limit to How Much Data We Collect?

Overall, this does raise an interesting question: If there is an ethical burden placed on any company when it has control of data and insights about customers, and since the function of a company is to sustain itself and be profitable (meaning it will never act principally in the consumers' interest), does that mean that companies should limit, whether voluntarily or through legislation, the amount of data they collect?

Some in the data security space talk about a model known as "focused collection," which is advocated by the White House's Consumer Data Privacy Bill of Rights. "Focused collection" prescribes collecting only what's needed from the consumer for the operations of the business.

This is sensible; and if companies undertake it voluntarily, it's great. And it does mean reduced risk for the company collecting the data. If they have less sensitive data, they're proportionally less vulnerable to attack and liability if their servers are compromised.

All of this also brings up questions of what the power dynamic should be between service provider and customer.

Of what I describe today, an awful lot of that kind of information becomes a kind of brokered power, and it could potentially and fundamentally change the relationship dynamic between company and customer.

Google and Facebook have extensive information about us, much more so than most people realize. Google owns the bulk of the advertising landscape distributed across the web, and they can track data across websites that use its AdSense product. Facebook has access to a great deal of that data, too, due to its advertisers and potential advertisers integrating a tracking "pixel," which passes data about user movement back to them.

We've already become culturally acclimated to the idea that we hand over a lot of data. As brand owners, designers, and data advocates, we often take for granted that customers, users, patients, students, and all of our constituents will hand over their data in exchange for our services. That is often true. But we're duty bound to be intentional in our obligation to be responsible, mindful of the ethical burden that data places on us, and respectful of the power and trust that is exchanged there.

***

We make the data points. We *are* the data points. We don't yet have a framework for how to treat and appreciate the richness of the humanity that's represented in those data points.

A framework for that must include a data model that acknowledges both relevance and discretion as respect. Relevance alone is an insufficient guide. Imagine that you blurted out everything you knew about everyone you knew in any setting. Pretty quickly, you would have no friends.

In a parallel way, marketers shouldn't expect more intimate insights than they need; and they can't expect to be able to play every card they've got all the time. Too much targeting goes beyond the filter bubble and starts to fatigue the customer.

Moreover, in designing projects and data models, it would really behoove companies to consider the data they'll truly need to collect.

I suppose it's too much to ask for companies to avoid collecting data that's right there in front of them, even if they don't need it; but it becomes an ethical burden when the company has access to unnecessary data that could easily be used to manipulate. Such is the case with Uber and their customers' battery levels.

Of course the data itself has no motive. It's only in the framework of the data collector's motive that it matters. Knowing whether you're an ex-smoker isn't terribly ethically burdensome in the context of encouraging a friend on Facebook who's quitting smoking by saying that you quit smoking ten years ago. But if that Facebook comment is visible to an entity that is harvesting that kind of information and passing it along to your health insurance provider, then what is that? In such cases, how can an insurance company be incentivized *not* to use that data, other than regulations that might restrict it? Market forces will want access to whatever data they can get.

This is why environmental tracking (such as beacons) presents such a quandary and such a need for this level of reflection. On one hand, there are potentially hundreds of legitimate use cases that can simplify customer experience and streamline company costs.

On the other hand, what a can of worms that opens up.

Adding Value Instead of Over-Optimizing

With all this data, there's going to be a very understandable inclination to try to optimize for everything. Organizations, however, aren't very good at optimizing along multiple dimensions, and humans who have to carry out the work of these distracted and distractible organizations get frustrated when they don't have clear direction.

There's a simple solution: Focus the organization around adding value to the human experience as it incrementally works its way toward improved experiences. Whatever products a company develops, whatever campaigns it launches, whatever communications it has with its customers, the underlying goal should be focusing upon the value in the relationship. Make the value clearer to prospective customers earlier on; remove value-diminishing parts of transacting with the company; and emphasize long-term value in existing customer relationships.

In practice, this often involves the same tactics that would be part of a more optimization-obsessed company-centric process—such as optimizing checkout flows to remove friction and increase conversion rate. But the tacit knowledge that comes from optimizing for value is subtly different from what comes from optimizing simply to optimize. A team can easily go off-mission in the latter scenario. Testing road maps are harder to prioritize. Conflicting data sets are harder to reconcile. But with an emphasis on building value in customer relationships, the team has confidence to navigate these scenarios.

***

Years ago, I was hired as managing director for a shop that was looking to evolve from design and SEO to more of a full-service digital marketing agency. Weeks before I'd been hired, they'd completed a website redesign for a client that offered marriage counseling retreats. In the first conference call I sat in on with this client, they were bringing up concern because they noticed that their website lead generation rate—which, in their case, meant completed inquiry forms from a person seeking help for a troubled marriage—had dropped precipitously since the redesign. No one could explain why: After all, the redesign followed what were considered industry best practices. It simplified the overall design, streamlined visitor access to the intake form, and cut the length of the intake form by more than half.

On paper, the agency had done everything right. But given the results, we had to step back and think differently about it. I started to wonder if efficiency was really what visitors to this website would really value most, or if in the interest of reassuring the visitors, we could afford to slow the process down. So we tested it. We reinstated the longer version of the form, still wrapped in a cleaner design; and as you may have guessed, conversion rate went back up. The longer, more narrative form—which included questions like, "When did you first start to notice problems in your marriage?"—may have given the inquiring visitor a sense of being cared for, a sense that they were entering therapy already. Moreover, it provided the retreat service more context when they followed up with the prospective attendee, giving the service a better chance to empathetically connect with the prospective clients.

At a glance, this story may not have anything to do with physical place or connected experiences, but it underscores a fundamental truth in dealing with humans. Our need to be shown respect can override our appreciation for things like efficiency, simplicity, or even low cost. If an interaction demonstrates respect, or even a proxy for respect—such as relevance, discretion, or modeled empathy through an immersive inquiry form—we are likely to recognize and appreciate it. It's easy to imagine what analogous connected experiences might look like. Perhaps messages or offers are targeted based on proximity alone, but they overstep the comfort a person has with the brand or service and the interaction fails. Connected experiences have tremendous opportunities to bypass respect and overplay their hands, so to speak.

Privacy and Data in Place

In the larger conversation about the convergence of physical and digital experience, and given what we know about our digital selves being our aspirational selves, it's critically important that we think about the role of privacy in experience design.

It's also worth considering that some new technologies come into our lives as opt-in, meaning we're outside the system until we choose to opt into it. Others come into our lives as opt-out, meaning we're in unless we say otherwise. Location tracking and targeting has largely entered public life in an opt-out model, in the sense that people buy sophisticated smartphones all the time and in their early iterations, location tracking was either on by default or ambiguously worded. People were using them as intended, which means they'd turn on location services, enable apps to use location, and then not necessarily connect the dots that the push notifications they got in the mall were because of the data they were voluntarily sharing.

Google was criticized for its location history in Android devices, mostly because the wording on the settings screen promised that the data was "anonymous" even though it was tied to the user's Google account.

Technologies like facial recognition present emerging privacy considerations and concerns, especially within the context of augmented reality and its potential widespread use.

There was a Google Glass app to identify emotions based on people's facial expressions and gender in 2014, and it could display this information in the user's augmented view.[26] There was even a surveillance video sharing program called Facewatch that integrated with security systems to identify people's likely emotional states.[27]

As ominous as some of this sounds, the underlying technology can be incredibly useful stuff in the right context. In later sections of this book, we'll explore using similar algorithms to tailor experiences and offers in ways people might consider worthwhile. The key, as a customer, as a citizen, and, yes, as a human, is that you have perceive sense of value (whether in the form of safety, convenience, or something else) in what you're signing up for in exchange for what you're disclosing.

The Convenience—Privacy—Access Relationship

People generally don't want to be bothered by messages or experiences that don't align with their existing motivations. And when asked, most will say that they don't want to give up their privacy or personal data.

But if you offer someone access to something restricted in exchange for their personal data, chances are, if it's interesting enough to them, they'll make the trade. There's a catch, though: They have to be reasonably assured that their security won't be compromised in making the trade.

There's a whole economy built around the principle of transparency in exchange for trust, of access in exchange for protection. Just because consumers are willing to give up information in the moment doesn't mean they always will, doesn't mean you're asking for the right level of detail, doesn't mean there won't be legislation in the future that restricts what you can collect and use.

Consumers need better education and better protection, and this is not that book. But business and organizations need better strategy to collect what is meaningful, use it respectfully, and guard it carefully. They need to organize a plan to collect what they're going to collect based on a sense of what can provide insights and maximum alignment, in order to create the most meaningful experiences.

That means thinking about the data model in new and different ways. It's subtle, but it might mean thinking about the underlying relationship between entities in your database.

There are strong relationships and weak relationships; some things need to be closely connected in the context of the business objectives overall, while other pieces of data are peripheral and incidental and can be modeled with separation to keep them from bogging down the data model.

For example, you may be collecting patient information in one context that pertains to your ability to contact the patient and follow up on appointments and scheduling. In another context, you may be collecting their medical history, reported symptoms, and test results. These need to be related, but their relationship should be carefully considered so that access to the different contexts can be controlled and safeguarded. I once heard Noah Harlan, a mobile technology entrepreneur and digital strategist, helpfully distinguish privacy and security by saying, "Privacy is who has unauthorized access to your data; security is who has authorized access to your data."

The Pew Research Center's report on customer privacy and data sharing demonstrates customers' complicated attitudes toward the data trade-off. The big question is what constitutes "tangible benefits" for customers:

While many Americans are willing to share personal information in exchange for tangible benefits, they are often cautious about disclosing their information and frequently unhappy about what happens to that information once companies have collected it. For example, when presented with a scenario in which they might save money on their energy bill by installing a "smart thermostat" that would monitor their movements around the home, most adults consider this an unacceptable tradeoff (by a 55% to 27% margin). As one survey respondent explained: *"There will be no 'SMART' anythings in this household. I have enough personal data being stolen by the government and sold [by companies] to spammers now.*[28]*"*

This is why people are willing to use Google's free email, despite a background level of awareness that their data might be used by Google. But when it comes to the data exchanged in physical spaces, people tend to get a little more creeped out.

The Pew study further demonstrates that context matters to people in terms of their comfort level with the exchange of data for access and security.

Certain realms are not inherently private and different rules about surveillance and sharing apply. Certain physical spaces or types of information are seen as inherently less private than others. One survey respondent noted how these norms influence his views on the acceptability of workplace surveillance cameras: *"It is the company's business to protect their assets in any way they see fit.*[29]

Social media is used primarily for people to communicate with friends. Yet social media ranks at the bottom of trust rankings:

Last week, while preparing a lecture, I searched quickly for some charts showing survey results for social media usage and privacy. The huge mismatch between what people want and what they are getting today was stunning. Social media I learned are used mainly for communicating with relatives and close friends with the next most significant use relating to political discourse. Yet social media was at the bottom of the trust rankings, with only 2 percent confidence. About 70 percent of respondents said they are very concerned about privacy and protection of their data.[30]

The problem with the model is that online advertising in particular relies heavily on transparent customer data. Once again, as the saying goes, if you're not paying for the product, you are the product. Consumers increasingly do know this, and where there are privacy concerns, some are taking protections. Some might set up fake email addresses and social media profiles to take advantage of certain offers without the risk of compromising their "real" data stores.

This complicates the advertising-supported business model, which relies on targeting offers to people who show an affinity for a certain idea or product. Security expert Tim Hwang argues,

The issue with privacy in particular is that the predominant business model for many of the companies that hold some of the most sensitive data online is based on advertising as the primary revenue model, which incentivizes companies to collect more data so they can use data more aggressively to promote adverts, to make more money and stay alive. Sometimes these companies will use the data in ways that their users may be uncomfortable with and one of the key challenges they face is how to balance advertisers and users, and the privacy implications of how they draw the line between the two.[31]

One of the less-cited but most valuable reasons for companies to strive for a meaningful approach to data collection and use is because it fosters an honest, authentic relationship between company and customer. The company that aligns its messaging and experiences with its motivations and the customers' motivations is setting the stage for a connection that promotes trust, and the customer who trusts the safety of the interaction is not guarded or misleading in their intentions. The customer data that is collected under those circumstances is bound to be cleaner and more informative.

Or, to return to Tim Hwang:

Authenticity is the common goal, both for users and for platforms. Authenticity is when you have struck the right balance of data collection and security measures. Users want to be authentic online, they want to feel like they are not constrained because they are being surveilled and they can't act in a way that they want. Platforms also want that because it provides them with valuable data. The data of a consumer that is actively hiding things from you is not going to be very useful data, particularly from an advertising standpoint.[32]

The thing is, we may say we're creeped out by data and technology, but if it's used to create compelling experiences, to anticipate our needs, to deliver value, and to do so with a sense of safety and privacy, very few of us will object.

So the mission is to develop an approach to handling consumer data, patient data, student data—all of it—in a way that offers the most value to the person while bringing the most value to your business. That's going to take some strategic planning. It's going to take an understanding of the underlying framework that drives those interactions.

We'll get there by looking more closely in the next chapter at how to think about place.

CHAPTER EIGHT

Metaphors: Digital Experience Through the Lens of Place

Thinking about digital experiences as virtual places is not new; many of the metaphors we use to describe online functions and interactions have been borrowed from the physical world. But applying these terms, like *traffic* or *page*, we carry over metaphorical associations in subtle ways. Examining these metaphors and their associations can give us new insights into what we've come to expect from digital spaces, and how to open up opportunities to create more integrated, connected experiences. We'll look more closely at them throughout this next section.

Metaphors: Experiencing One Thing in Terms of Another

Neuroscience has learned that we make meaning through activating parts of our brains associated with the idea we're processing. For example, when you read the phrase "Sam ate a delicious steak," it's not only the areas of your brain that deal with semantics and syntax that get involved. The area of your brain associated with taste gets involved, too.

That may seem obvious in retrospect, but it's an important point. It shows that on some level, we really do *experience* the meaning we interpret. And when we hear metaphors, we aren't just taking a figurative picture for granted; we're actually using the parts of our brains associated with the figurative idea to process the meaning.

Metaphors, then, constitute an incredibly important part of experience design.

Legacy Metaphors

When was the last time you dialed your phone? No, really: When did you last *dial* any phone? The term *dial* came to us from the rotary phone interface, which was largely phased out by push-button phones in the 1970s and '80s. If you're under forty, chances are you've never even seen a rotary phone in person, much less dialed one. Yet the word lives on.

Even once we began using push-button phones, no one ever really talked about "pushing" phone numbers. Now perhaps we might say we "tap" them but nobody says that; we still "dial."

For that matter, your smartphone isn't much of a "phone"; at least, it isn't primarily a phone for most of us, who use it more for email and texting and things other than making and receiving calls. Yet the "phone" nomenclature lives on.

If you truly took inventory of all of the interaction metaphors you encounter on a daily basis, you'd probably be surprised by how many of them—either the interaction itself or the words we use to describe it— are based on outdated technology.

For instance, you've probably seen an image of a 3.5-inch floppy disk used as an icon to mean "Save" far more recently than you've seen an actual 3.5-inch floppy disk. After all, that's how we used to save our work in progress . . . twenty years ago. But then, what would be a more contemporary metaphor? A fluffy cloud (another beleaguered metaphor)? Would the image of a cloud adequately convey that the implied action is "save"? Would that association be reassuring, or would it cause people to hesitate and wonder how safe their data is out in some fluffy cloud? And of course, *the cloud* is itself a metaphor that represents—wait for it—a series of connected disks.

Perhaps these legacy metaphors give us a comforting feeling of being anchored in a stable experience, even as the devices themselves evolve. Perhaps we crave the familiarity of the old even as we constantly update to the new. Or perhaps we just don't give it that much thought.

Metaphors in Marketing

* * *

But even more tangible than these deep metaphors in our surroundings are the analogies we often use in marketing that convey associations we may or may not be intending.

For example, let's say you operate a computer repair business. In order to explain to people what you do, you could compare it to being a mechanic or being a brain surgeon. Not to knock mechanics, but certainly the latter analogy makes the work look more specialized and expert, while the former analogy is perhaps more approachable and friendly. The analogy you choose to use depends on what characteristics you want to connect to the work you do.

Whatever the case, our businesses demand that we be more thoughtful with those brand associations. It's not enough to rely on the easiest or most familiar metaphor if that's not the one that carries the meaning you want your business to have.

Even the way you organize products and information within your business, and the taxonomies you use throughout your business are a kind of metaphor. They describe the framework of your brand's worldview, as the linguist George Lakoff so vividly demonstrated with the title of his 1987 book, *Women, Fire, and Dangerous Things.*[33] Subtle cues, such as the placement of items relative to one other, can signal meaningful differences. If you're stocking a craft supply store targeting hobbyists, you might choose to organize paintbrushes with paints to make selection easy and accessible for people just starting out. If you're stocking an art supply store aimed at professionals, on the other hand, you may want to organize paintbrushes with other tools and paints with other pigments to convey depth and breadth of selection and an appreciation of the importance of the right tools. These may seem like trivial nuances, but nuances convey our biases. Our biases make up our brands, and good brands are opinionated.

The way you organize content on your website, merchandise in your store, and all your interactions says more about you to customers than you may realize. This is why all of this matters: because meaning is about connection and relevance. The metaphors you use in your marketing say just as much as the words that make up your copy, if not more. It's worth taking the time to review your marketing and your overall customer experience to make sure what you *are* saying is what you really mean to say.

***

In order to have that rich conversation, though, in order to dig deep into what we mean when we think about the richness of the opportunities of the integration layers, I think it's really important to think about the ways that we perceive and experience the physical world and the digital world, in a sense. What are the models, the frameworks that we use mentally to really experience those things so that we can try to bring them more in line and more together. I think it's important to go to the study of metaphor. It's really about meaning, and where there's meaning in the experiences of things, in the data we use to describe those things.

A lot of my work over time has been about meaning, even when it has been in web technology, content management, digital strategy, and marketing. My educational background was in languages and linguistics, so it comes naturally to me to have meaning be along for the ride in how we communicate and how we think about the underpinnings of what we are conveying to one another.

So metaphors are a really handy kind of reveal for what we're actually saying about something at a different layer, a more subconscious layer, what;s happening below the surface when we talk about a thing.

There are metaphors we have used to describe physical space and digital space and some of those overlap so I think it's really important to examine that.

In doing this, I look back to another book by George Lakoff (and Mark Johnson) called "Metaphors we Live By." There's a quote that I think really summarizes why metaphor is a relevant tool for this type of work:

> The essence of metaphor is understanding and experiencing one kind of thing in terms of another.
> — George Lakoff[34] (emphasis mine)

So it's not just about *describing* one thing as another thing, and it's not just about using analogies in language, or about the poetic use of language; it's more that it actually is experienced that way. It isn't coincidence there are terms that describe online concepts in the language of offline constructs, but that those offline constructs have actually informed our understanding of the online concepts. The thing you are describing in terms of another thing is now experienced as if it is that other thing at some level in your mind and in the minds of those with whom you communicate.

The Metaphors of How We Experience Digital as Place

It's unsurprising, then, that we have a series of metaphors to describe digital concepts in terms of place. It is important to understand how we conceive of the experiences we intend for human beings to have in digital spaces, and how many of them already borrow from metaphors of physical place.

Data as metaphor, metaphor as experience

When you decide that you want to track the entry into a website, an "add to cart," a checkout, and the exit, you have defined a shape to that experience; and that shape is preset by the company's preferences and what, to the company, determines success. But the customer has a happy path, too, and it may look different. Perhaps the shape of that path would be to enter on meaningful content, which helps the customer identify their next step; to consume enough content to feel empowered, but not too much to feel annoyed; and to complete the transaction with ease. There are qualifiers to each of those steps that have to do with qualitative experiences, and they're more subjective than readily available metrics (including visits, purchases, and conversion rates).

If we stop and review the ideal metaphor from the customer—or better yet, from the human—point of view, the experience might look different. For the human on the other side of the interaction, the appropriate shopping metaphor might be conquest. It might be discovery. It might be satisfaction, or comfort, or any number of other constructs that could dramatically affect the way they view the experience. Their perspective could mean that the way you view the experience and the way they view the experience is misaligned.

Strive to be human when interacting with humans.

In any given situation, it may be helpful to ask yourself, "What would a human-to-human interaction look like?" How would you (or the appropriate person) conduct your end of the interaction?

We Can Start With This Metaphor About Place:

@ Is a metaphor of place

We have a metaphor that we use all the time probably without thinking about it as place, but the @ symbol tells us where someone is, what entity someone is associated with, that has some kind of takeaway for thinking about the nodes and structures of digital life. This is part of an address, which is itself a metaphor of place. This is how we find someone.

Metaphors and Metadata

There's an interesting link between metaphors and metadata. You need the metaphor to determine what metadata is relevant. You need the metadata to describe the experience of the metaphor.

Take for example, music streaming. The literal process is just a file stored on a server being accessed by a client and decoded through software that interprets the encoding as audio. But in order to make that experience meaningful, the packaging of that process is described in terms that are skeuomorphic: They refer back to the older experience of listening to music on a hi-fi record player, through the radio, or recorded on a CD. The visual icon that stands in for a song often depicts a vinyl record or a CD. But even beyond the iconography, when we think about "skipping" a track or "fast-forwarding" through it, we're invoking the experiences of bygone music listening technology because we're familiar with it. We still have "albums" in music, even though most listeners are not listening by the album. (Artists are, however, making more money from vinyl sales than from streaming.[35] But that's a discussion for another book.) Spotify and other services have "radio" features that play content related in some way to a starter seed, like a song or an artist.

Since we need these metaphors for people to understand the experience of music streaming, we also need to model the metadata around the metaphors. There are "albums" in digital music, which serve only as bundles of creative work. To optimize the services, we'll want insights about how many people skipped a track.

Because digital music playback and even streaming music have now been around long enough to breed listener/user familiarity, the playback interfaces have started to break away from the skeuomorphs and use broader metaphors of music and of file interaction.

***

When you think about data models, there are always relationships between the different entities in the model. The relationship between the entities describes how they interact, but it also hints at underlying assumptions and metaphor:

Employees work in a department
Teachers teach students
A car is a type of vehicle

There's often also metaphor embedded in the nature of the relationship, and that metaphor influences the shape of the data collection.

For example, a song is part of . . . an album? A playlist? A radio station? A collection? A catalog? A library? I could keep going. There are many ways to think about one entity in its relationship to others, and the way we describe it is likely to affect our thinking about the shape and dimensions and limitations of it. The data point or entity exists not just on its own, but as it is *experienced in context*. So it's important that we're mindful of the context we're creating, the meaning we're shaping, with the metaphors we accept and design into our products, our messaging, and our strategies.

The Evolution of Place Metaphors Online

It's important for the purposes of this discussion to remember that in the early days of the World Wide Web, the idea of the home page generally referred to our own individual pages that we created and maintained to express our identity and preferences. It generally included a list of links we thought important, and the functional intent was to serve as our own customized jumping-off point into the rest of the web.

But as time went on, three things happened in parallel: The web became more commercial, so more and more companies developed web pages and sites; browsers started offering a feature whereby the user could set their "home" page to any page; and the web grew in popularity among non-techie people, so more and more people got online who didn't necessarily have the skills or resources to create a home page of their own.

Return to "Home Page"

So by 2016, a semantic shift has fully taken place where the idea of the "home page" is largely understood to mean the conceptual root page of a website that anchors the brand and directs traffic to categories and topical areas within the content of the site. It's the place where a company like Apple asserts its Apple-ness before sending users off down trails specific to Macs or iPhones or customer support. If you view the web through the lens of one of these big brand presences, then "home page" is not so functionally far-off from the original notion.

But for individuals, it's a vastly different experience. Most web users do not have a personal website, and thus do not have that original meaning of "home page."

Why is this important?

Well, when we think about the notion of home, we will see that within that idea there is the idea of controlling your space and having the ability to control your experiences. Home to many people means the place where they are most in charge of creating their own experiences. That has a lovely symmetry with the initial idea of the personal home page, but in the current state of web usage, the idea of home has no widespread parallel.

We need to understand the way people perceive their journeys online. And in order to understand that, we need to understand the way they perceive their starting points.

If there is no home, there is no anchor, nowhere to wander away from and to return to; so our wanderings become constant, we have no sense of continuity, and we may lack identity relative to what we experience.

Home is also at once a human idea and an animal need. In a Maslow-esque hierarchy of needs, home is both fundamental and aspirational. We need a basic version of home to survive, but we also constantly seek its ideal. Home is sacred to us; if it is robbed, we feel violated.

Somewhat similarly, we feel violated if our digital identity or information is compromised. Our digital spaces have qualities of home about them, too. In parallel ways to how our digital selves are our aspirational selves, as discussed in the earlier section "Our Digital Selves," it may be that our digital spaces *are* our aspirational homes.

Why do our digital metaphors convey place? What is the purpose or benefit?

We can all relate to spatial experiences. We have "windows," entrances, exits, "pages," of which there are "landing" pages, "home" pages, and then "traffic," which we "drive" to the "sites" we have "built."

With 3-D printing and wearable tech, the lines between online and offline experiences are starting to blur and will only continue to do so. And as that happens, we're going to need a cleaner and more intentional understanding of what place does for us in experiences, and how we can be intentional about creating it.

Digital landscapes have been thought of in a physical context since Richard Saul Wurman coined the term "information architects" in 1975. It seemed natural to link the idea of architecture and the idea of information organization—and that was nearly twenty years before the

World Wide Web existed.

Now, in 2016, Rem Koolhaas has made the same observation, but with the explicit recognition of metaphor:

Architecture and the language of architecture—platform, blueprint, structure—became almost the preferred language for indicating a lot of phenomenon that we're facing from Silicon Valley. They took over our metaphors, and it made me think that regardless of our speed, which is too slow for Silicon Valley, we can perhaps think of the modern world maybe not always in the form of buildings but in the form of knowledge or organization and structure and society that we can offer and provide.[36]

What's stopping us from using other metaphors online? Shoes, walking, running, doors, shelves, books? It may seem like a silly thought, but expanding our thinking about the metaphors we use can open new possibilities for innovative experiences.

Traffic, Cost, and the Nuance of Metaphor

We have a whole set of metaphors that describe digital experience as travel or motion. We talk about **traffic**, about the customer's **journey**, about **mapping** that journey, and about the user's **path**. We also have the idea of **landing**, as a landing page on a website—the first page a user visits on the website, and even this concept of **visiting** a website is a metaphor of place.

When we talk about "traffic" to a website, it sounds like the "traffic" of highways and city streets, but it actually borrows from the retail need to measure "foot traffic" in stores—meaning the number of shoppers in and out the doors of the store in a given day or time period.

But the mechanics of setting foot in a store are both like and unlike viewing an e-commerce website, in ways that are helpful to break down.

Ways in which the concepts are alike:

- They are human-centric, or human-experience-centric.
- They deal with volume.
- They deal with access.

* * *

Ways in which the concepts differ:

- The experience of a store is linear; a person can't jump from point to point.
- People don't multitask as easily or as much in physical retail stores as they do when online.
- The effort required by a person to visit a physical store is generally much higher than that required to visit a website.

It can be hard to disambiguate these terms and the physical entities they reference from how we think about them in the digital context, but as you step back and take those words at their more common parlance—physical use—you realize how much of the physical world has colored the experience of attributes in the digital space.

And those origins are interesting to delve into, because if you look at a metaphor like traffic and the concept it describes, we know that the most common usage of traffic, in the physical world, is road congestion, and is something to be endured. Of course the web usage owes more to the concept of "foot traffic" in a store, but it's still helpful to explore what we have meant throughout time when we think about this metaphor, and what lessons might be applicable today for what we do with it.

Also, the concept of traffic online is applied to more than just e-commerce websites; so all websites, even informational websites, spend considerable effort measuring and maximizing their "foot traffic"—which may not be the metaphorical aspect that will benefit them most.

Years ago, I owned a digital strategy and analytics agency, and my clients often wanted to know about how to "increase the traffic" to their websites. They asked this as if they made no distinction in the kind of traffic they got to their site.

I always find that interesting, since in the physical world, when we think about traffic, it's always a negative.

In fact, even online, traffic is a cost. You're bringing the people in from somewhere, and you're paying for them to come. You're paying for the bandwidth to serve them content.

So yes, that traffic does come at a cost to you.

That's not to say that traffic is bad, of course. It's just that recognizing the cost of the traffic can help create a disciplined mindset around marketing.

When you flip the idea that traffic is desirable, and amend that to traffic is expensive, and that we need to be mindful about the makeup and management of that traffic, then we achieve more parity in the metaphor, and it's potentially informative and useful to us.

Every time we see a metaphor borrowed from one context into another, it's helpful to remind ourselves about the relationships between these ideas and what subtle connotations they convey. Because there's too often too much that we lose to the everyday because words become mundane, but they still trigger associations on subconscious levels.

Movement Versus Stillness

I grew up in a small south suburb of Chicago, and my early memories of my family making day trips into the city are filled with fascination at the pulse of movement. The pedestrians filled the sidewalks along Michigan Avenue, the buses and taxis and cop cars and bicyclists and everything bustled, and it all happened with a determination and energy that to me felt far more alive than the suburbs ever did.

In a related way, you can think about relationships of digital and physical metaphors as having different dimensions to them, where some of them relate to movement—such as flow or journey—and others relate to stillness—such as bookmark or save.
- metaphors of movement: flow, journey
- metaphors of stillness: bookmark, save

Part of the experience, as well, with cities and other places is in your sense of movement through them. And perhaps part of their meaning to you.

Movement Through Space

Although Times Square would certainly be considered by many measures to be a very successful place, the flow of visitors through the space was inhibitive, and locals tended to avoid it. The subtle efforts made by the architectural firm to improve those issues are a classic example of placemaking as well as a vivid illustration of intentionality about movement through place.

Beginning in 2011, the Norwegian architectural firm Snøhetta undertook a revamp of Times Square to make the space easier to move through. (David Owen wrote a beautiful profile about it in the *New Yorker* in 2013.[37]) One of the constraints of the space, as one of the firm's partners described it, was how in addition to the pulsating energy of the brightly lit and dynamic billboards, the space itself, due to the shape created by Broadway's diagonal intersections around 45th Street, creates a sense of constriction as people move through it.

On the other side of town, the architects noted that the information kiosk in the center of Grand Central Terminal seemed to break up the immensity of the space and create a fluidity of movement; so they decided to try something similar in Times Square. In addition, they reasoned that if a person is walking toward you, there's a tension created of who's going to move, who gives way first; but if your obstacle is not a person but a stationary object, you know who gives way. (Obviously, you do.) As part of their solution they added a series of long granite benches —fixed objects, which also serve as occasional seating. Their addition encourages a more natural movement through the space, and it turns out that it creates less tension too.

So the question this poses as you think about the design of integrated experience is: What is the nature of the experience that you want someone to have in the setting of your website, application, or system? And how does it relate to the sense of place it's connected to? What sense of momentum or reflection best serves the overall experience of the store, hospital, or museum you're designing for? Do you want to create a sense of comfort, or is there perhaps some reason to create a sense of energy or even unrest? What will be the appropriate feeling to invoke? Moreover, how can the data model reinforce that? It may need to be able to measure senses of motion or stillness, or whatever dimension is meaningful at any given time to know whether that design intent is effective.

Metaphors of Digital Experience as Printed Matter

At the outset of the World Wide Web, it was perhaps an obvious metaphor to think about web content as printed reading material, which meant at least the following metaphors:

- pages
- bookmark

The terminology has stuck, even though what happens on "pages" could be video content, an app, or some other highly interactive experience.

But it's still helpful to think about this metaphor of reading and what reading is about—that is to say, reading is about relaying information in a way that's linear, and/or archived, and/or easily referenced.

When understood, that metaphor can inform that digital experience; and the data model can support it when that's relevant. In other words, if there need to be aspects of metadata that have to do with findability and retrievability to enhance this kind of experience, that's where we might want to go with our ideation.

The Data Layer of the Experience

You have to design for the data layer of the experience. For example, if you're creating an experience that builds from the metaphor of reading, it's helpful to think through the metaphor (without being skeuomorphic) in order to understand the data and metadata you will need to collect to optimize that experience.

If the experience is meant to be metaphorically like a book, you're optimizing for deep engagement with the written content; so you'll probably want to know about page turns.

If the experience is meant to be metaphorically like a newspaper, you're optimizing for currency and authority/influence of content; so you'll want to know about clipping and sharing.

Thinking through the experience associated with the metaphor can help unearth not only where there are opportunities to take the experience deeper but also what data to collect in order to optimize.

Metaphors of Digital Experience as Architecture or a Building

* * *

Whether you're designing it, analyzing it, or using it, a website's parallels to a building are very graspable; and the related metaphors can be quite useful in visualizing and dimensionalizing digital space. Even before the World Wide Web, we knew that computers had "windows." That paradigm of conceptualizing the presentation of information on a screen has persisted for decades in operating systems and software applications. But the web also gave us:

- Entrances
- Exits

The ideas of architecture have long influenced digital space. Even the term *information architecture* makes that clear.

So we have these metaphors of digital experience as a building: entrances, exits, and windows. Which makes me start questioning, what are the elements we're not using?

Going Beyond the Obvious

What are other characteristics of a building? What might they suggest about experience?

You could apply this question to any of the categories of metaphor, but for example, what are the other characteristics of a building that we don't use in describing digital experiences?

Doors?

Stairs?

Floors?

Roof?

Ceiling?

Could there be anything useful about these ideas?

If we were to think about the concept of, say, "doors" as a digital metaphor, what might that mean? Doors are transitions between one room and the next, so what might that suggest about experience design, and how we facilitate a meaningful experience through doors for users?

If we were to think about "stairs," is there a connective metaphor between levels, between access points? Is there something there that allows us to flatten out some part of a journey?

In other words, with any of these ideas, can we borrow from our metaphorical thinking about design in order to broaden our minds? What are the available tools we can use to think about design and data in such a way that we can provide these new, different, and meaningful experiences?

Rethinking the Metaphors

What we have is the language of place and the lens of context. We learn from observing the way the language of place has infiltrated digital to think about local coherence and how the idea performs in context.

When we use the words of a place to describe a digital experience, we are infusing that experience with dimension that gives shape to the abstract and expands our ability to conceive of the digital world. But if we use the words sloppily, or choose words or ideas that limit the experience unnecessarily, we may miss out on opportunities to innovate.

Take for example Netflix. You probably know, as most people do, that Netflix was all about renting unlimited DVDs before pivoting into streaming. What you may not know is that before launching that DVD subscription program, they started out as a service to rent DVDs a la carte—just like Blockbuster, except online and through the mail. (I joined the company just as they were retiring the a la carte model.) When they hit upon the idea of a DVD subscription model, they discovered that they had been working with a rapidly-aging notion of how customers wanted to interact with the physical world; and their new model simplified it. Of course their even newer model—streaming video—simplified it even more. What are the wide-open opportunities to rethink the interactions with the customers in your market?

It's key to remember that the convergence of physical and digital happens around the human experience. It's not a new phenomenon, but the opportunities to adapt and offer more contextually relevant experiences are evolving all the time.

More and more we're going to have amplified data, which will allow us to create many rich experiences if we're mindful of them.

The Language of Relative Place and Movement

We've already explored the role sense plays in making meaning. But one of the most overlooked senses in design is the kinesthetic—dealing with the importance of movement through space. That sense of space is in full play with technology when it comes to gesture-based interfaces and other haptics. The accelerometer in our smartphones has an idea of which way we're moving, how fast, and at what elevation. Right now that data is being used mostly for navigation apps and games, but it will become part of more and more interfaces.

It matters, then, to think about the way we think about movement.

Once we've looked at metaphors in that way, as digital experience has borrowed from physical place, there's also some worthwhile considerations of the language of place, some of which has also started to be used in digital experience. Examining place language could also reveal interesting thought-provoking tools for us as we think about converged digital and physical experiences.

It's been something of a hobby of mine to collect examples of place in language, and one of the things that interests me most about them is how many convey changing perspective, movement, or relative place.

Look at these words, for example:

- *parallax*: the effect of place and perspective on what's visible or in focus
- *deixis*: the perspective of place (or time or person) in language ("here" versus "there," or "this" versus "that")
- itinerant: wandering, especially for work
- *peripatetic*: wandering
- and then . . . *proximity*

There are so many wonderfully rich words about perspective and viewpoint, and you have to examine how they relate to the place, in the sense that you have a different way of looking at things by standing in a different place. They're all about movement, perspective, and relationship to place.

The first one on the list, *parallax*, is a term we've seen these last few years in front-end web design to describe elements that appear to be moving independently of one another. But in a physical sense, parallax has to do with the effect of place and perspective on what's visible or in focus. So we've already borrowed that into digital usage, but I think there's even more that it could tell us about the way we experience the world. There's so much about what is in focus or visible given obstacles in one's path, given your place in space and time, or what you're trying to see or understand, that it can describe what is available for you to view or to comprehend. This could be a helpful way to think about complex and overwhelming information; but the idea of parallax could help us consider how to create the right perspective, or a just-enough perspective for people who are using a system.

For example if we have data that determines our rate of movement and can deduce whether we're driving or walking through a city, and if we know that each mode will have different kinds of obstacles and different kinds of opportunities, then the kinds of things that might be presented to us as options for our next actions—such as promotions or resources—might vary.

Another term on this list that I think is potentially helpful is *deixis*, which is a linguistic construct that describes the perspective of place in language. A great example is Airbnb's "Don't Go There; Live There" campaign (which we will discuss at length in "The Human-Centric Data Model: A Look at Airbnb's "Don't Go There; Live There" Campaign").

These are all potentially rich terms, with many nuances about movement and place that could relate to perspective and experience. Any of these might be good tools to prompt original thought about the design and data models needed for creating a satisfying experience.

Connected Ideas and the Metaphor of Curation

The web is the best interface we've had yet for exposing the connective layers of ideas—until something better comes along, perhaps. But for now, we're still reaping the benefits of living in a time when the links between ideas can be made visual and can be "explored," to use a physical metaphor.

Curation

The idea of curation is a metaphor borrowed from the art world, of course. Once I saw a world-class curator give a lecture, after the notion of "curated" social media had become a thing, and it nearly moved me to tears to think of the meaning he was adding to the experience of art.

The contemporary usage of the term curation, though, as it relates to digital content and social media, loosens the use of this terminology. Erin Kissane wrote an "epic" five-part series examining the notion of curation, differentiating between the kind of curation that implies filtering or selecting and the kind of curation that implies collection or preservation, but also digging deep into the cultural implications of extending the term.[38]

Still, no doubt there are digital art projects and "galleries" that merit the designation of being curated, but for general purposes, the pictures most of us are adding to our Pinterest accounts are only connected to the core idea of curation in the loosest possible way.

I don't find that troubling, and neither should you. After all, re-pinning pictures of sidewalk cafés in the Left Bank to my "Paris" board in Pinterest is no more removed from art museum curation than browsing on the web is from idly walking through a shopping center with no intent to buy.

When Online Goes Offline

It hasn't happened as much yet, but some metaphors have gone the other way: Ideas about how we experience digital life have started to trickle back over into a more physical/spatial usage. The connected dimension of our digital lives is separate enough from our physical lives that we understand the metaphor of "disconnecting" ourselves from the digital stream so that we can fully experience the physical side. The metaphorical notion of "offline" as the opposite counterpart to "online" has colored our understanding of context. We talk about "going offline" or taking a discussion "offline."

People occasionally speak hashtags aloud and use other internet memes colloquially. I hear people say "hashtag-first-world-problem" in informal social settings, and occasionally hear other spoken variants of internet cultural memes. Similarly, I hear people jokingly say "Delete!" when referring to something they want to stop.

URLs appear everywhere, on ads, in stores, in the dentist office; and social icons show up everywhere, too, although this is often a rather funny faux pas. The icon in print, without the context of the username or profile of the given social network, is fairly useless except as a general reminder to a would-be customer or fan that the entity exists on that social network, and the customer or fan should search them out to engage with them. As difficult as it is to acquire interested prospective customers and fans, that's a lot to ask, and it's not likely to happen in most cases.

It's increasingly common to see hashtags promoted as part of user generated content campaigns within brand advertising, such as #ShareACoke. And in turn, these can become promoted trends, often used in offline advertising such as billboards, bringing the convergence of this online content with its offline context and online promotion full circle and then some.

As yet, though, the metaphors of the digital world haven't made as much impact on physical placemaking. The physical world, though—the world we've all known all our lives—has been consciously *and* unconsciously woven into every dimension of online space.

Maps: Mapping Physical Place Versus Maps of Experience:

Empathy Maps, Journey Maps

Journey maps, strategy maps, empathy maps: We seem to rely a great deal on the notion of maps for guidance. Perhaps that's understandable given their history of guiding us through space. But clearly our relationship with maps extends beyond the cartographic and into the abstract conceptual.

Even maps that describe the physical world differ in their approach to fidelity to spatial relationships versus system relationships. Try navigating the New York City subway using a street map and you may well find it challenging, whereas the subway system map removes the context that isn't needed—the street grid and above-ground landmarks—and places emphasis upon what matters in the moment for the subway rider. But likewise, if you try to navigate the streets of New York City on foot using a subway map, you'll be at a loss for necessarily detail.

A successful map shows the relationships between points in a system using only the context layer that matters. It's a great example of what I call "relevance as a form of respect": Any more detail than needed could bog down the viewer or detract from the clarity of the relationships that matter.

So the scope of, say, a strategy map is only the relationships between elements needed to successfully understand the strategy. It doesn't need the details that matter at the tactical implementation level; those would only confuse matters.

Breadcrumbs

There's another interesting metaphor used in digital that is borrowed from the physical world, and it relates to this discussion: **breadcrumbs**.

What we're referring to culturally when we talk about breadcrumbs is the fairytale "don't get lost in the woods" sense. Which is also a pretty relevant idea when you think about someone navigating an unfamiliar website. The further and deeper they get into it, the more helpful it can be to have a way to trace their way back out. Yet we also know that digital experience is not a linear footpath, and it does not look like a carefully laid out journey map.

Those journey maps of our websites and mobile apps and digital presences and so on are really just flattened abstractions of a complex relationship of ideas, anyway, with access points we don't always plan for; and they are often presented in language that represents our thinking, not the visitor's.

What breadcrumbs can help us do is to be mindful of the humanistic element of context and how a user is coming into that experience, and what additional context of physical space or of background or of desire or confusion or whatever else is going on potentially in that person's real life as they interact with your flattened abstraction of how you want the thing to go down.

***

* * *

A customer journey map is an abstraction of the encounters and interactions a customer has with a brand—from awareness through some desired post-purchase state, such as referral, renewal, or retirement from the process. It's a figurative overlay of digital (and sometimes physical) experience, presented through the physical metaphor of linear progress through a journey. That journey is presented in an idealized sequence because to try to account for the variations on every customer's experience would render the map useless.

Speaking of maps, it's also interesting that when we look at GIS data, we're looking at a literal overlay of data and place.

When you have sensors connected to machinery, or even to discrete parts of machinery, you have the potential for vast amounts of data that can be used predictively to determine when equipment might break down, but with visualization on a map, you also get geographical patterns of usage. Departments of Transportation (DOTs) in states like Iowa have equipped their snowplows with sensors and communication equipment, and they departments can keep tabs on the fleet relative to weather forecasts so that they can be most prepared, effective, and efficient with salt application and snow removal.[39] They've even made that data publicly accessible in their Track a Plow website, which lets drivers know which roads have most recently been cleared.

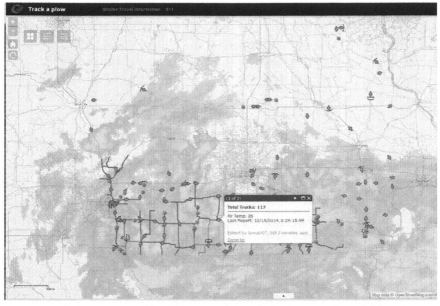

Image source: http://www.transportationmatters.iowadot.gov/

There are many ways maps can guide us through experience, and in our exploration of integrated experiences, they route together several relevant concepts: directions and navigation, as we discussed earlier in "Traffic, Cost, and the Nuance of Metaphor," GPS, as discussed in "Senses in Place; Sense and Technology," and how we give directions, as we'll discuss in "Humanlike Nuances."

And because of what maps demonstrate about context and layered experience of place, they also lead us perfectly into the next discussion: an examination of how augmented reality affects our experience of place.

CHAPTER NINE

Reality, Virtual Reality, Augmented Reality

Nowhere do the layers of pixels and place come together more than in the realms of augmented reality and virtual reality. The two are not really the same, but they deserve consideration together because they both pertain to the sensory experience of a "place" that doesn't exist without the aid of technology.

> Augmented reality and virtual reality both
> pertain to the sensory experience of a "place" that
> doesn't exist without the aid of technology.

Augmented reality is where you can still see your natural surroundings but you are also interacting through a screen layer, often transposed through a camera view of the surroundings. In other words, you might be holding your phone up in front of you, looking at your living room, and on your phone screen you see your living room with a chair you're thinking about buying.

Pokémon GO is augmented reality. IKEA has an augmented reality app for its catalog. Google Glass was an augmented reality wearable device.

What distinguishes virtual reality from augmented reality, primarily, is how immersive the experience is. At the moment, virtual reality is mostly experienced through goggles or a headset, sometimes with attached earpieces for accompanying audio, and is presented with alternate surroundings. Most VR experiences focus on immersion of sight and hearing, but some also involve gloves or other hand-related wearables that deal with your sense of touch, using vibrations and other haptic feedback. But augmented reality is basically a screen layer over the physical world, and it can be achieved in a wide range of ways.

Google is even experimenting with blended virtual and augmented. It has the potential to create amazingly rich experiences. In some cases, they may be experiences that we as users/customers/visitors can feel more in control of. In the meantime, there are already some worthwhile integrations of the physical and digital experience through both augmented reality and virtual reality, which we'll examine in the following sections.

Experiencing Place with Augmentation

We've established that the meaning and experience of a place is at least partly dependent on sensory experience. Since augmentation affects our sensory perception (at least what we see, and maybe other senses in the future), then to what extent is the meaning of that place altered by the augmentation?

How does the experience of a place change when it's augmented? What characteristics does a place take on, and how does it affect the meaning of that place?

The experience of a place through augmentation changes the sense of the place. Augmentation fundamentally changes that sense and potentially also changes the function of the place by adding a functional or descriptive layer over top of the physical layer. That can be very helpful in interpretation, museums or monuments.

Augmentation is starting to be used a great deal in retail, museums, and games (see the next section on "Augmented Reality Games"). It's also growing within branding and advertising, mainly through apps like Blippar, bringing ads into a physical experience.

Augmented Place and Community

You may be connected to other people who are likewise experiencing the surroundings in an augmented way, but you may be disconnected physically.

On the other hand, augmented reality is typically experienced through a camera lens or viewfinder that does not obscure surroundings, so as opposed to virtual reality, the user of the technology is not disconnected from other people who are not connected through the same technology.

Augmented Place and Identity

As you become part of the place for other people, your presence may be augmented as well. If you are able to understand what you might have in common with people in your vicinity, and they may be better able to understand what you might have in common with them, then your augmented identity overlaps the augmented experience of the place. There are, of course, privacy considerations and concerns with augmenting experience to include personal information, and the full impact of those considerations is just coming to light.

Augmented Place and Culture

Augmentation, in a sense, enhances the metadata of place, surfaces otherwise invisible connections. This can amplify cultural and historical artifacts and connect people who are viewing it in to others in dimensional ways across time and space.

As I wrote in an earlier section, "Chapter Five - The Meaning of Place," when we talk about meaning, we are looking for significance: "In thinking about what place means, we are looking for clues about what a place conveys into context, what signifiers it brings with it."

Sometimes significance is subtle, and it may take something external to make us realize what is significant about a place. When our perception of place is augmented by a layer of technology, the significance may be brought to the surface. The augmentation can expose a layer of significance and connectedness of surroundings that it might have taken us a long time to find.

If we were to experience a park, for example, with an augmented reality app that can identify types of trees, wildflowers, rocks, and other nature, might it surprise us with how much biodiversity surrounds us? Might we be struck by that, and be more likely to feel protective of it?

Or say we experience a retail store with the assistance of an augmented reality app or device. AR technology could be very helpful in guiding shoppers to the items they're looking for, or offering them alternatives based on their known history and patterns as well as inventory and availability. If the technology helps us discover a product we love, might it increase our loyalty to the store where we found the product?

Augmented Reality Games

As I write this, *Pokémon GO* is the biggest thing taking over the internet. The internet is awash in opinions about every aspect of the game, its growing player base, and its social implications.

In the first few days after it was released, there were stories about people complaining of sore calves because they did so much walking. *Pokémon GO* did what several generations of wearable fitness trackers failed to do: It got people outside and moving around.

It's no surprise that a gamification approach to getting people to move dramatically amplifies the effectiveness. But that probably wasn't exactly Niantic's strategy with *Pokémon GO*, either. Their strategy was presumably to build on the platform that had already been being built with Ingress and other apps and wrap a popular game around it. *Pokémon GO* just fit.

What's more interesting about it, though, is the sweeping changes it brings with it: new marketing models, opportunities with augmented reality, location-based marketing, and assorted issues with data privacy and security. The most interesting things about *Pokémon GO* have nothing to do with the game itself and everything to do with how different things are becoming and are continuing to be.

Connected Experiences Bring New Marketing Models

The marketing models are poised to be totally different now that an online interaction can be credibly and consistently traced to offline visits in stores. See the McDonald's deal with *Pokémon GO* to make all three thousand of its Japanese stores "gyms" in the game. The full details of their deal haven't been disclosed, but one option this presents is an incredible opportunity for cost-per-visit modeling.

* * *

Connected Experiences and Social Interaction

The social experiences are different with augmented reality, when interacting with a digital experience doesn't automatically mean being oblivious to the world around you. (Although obviously it still can. See, for example, the guys who fell off a cliff while playing *Pokémon GO*, or the person who drove into a cop car.)

But since you can engage with the game through a camera view of what's ahead of you, it's actually possible to walk and play and still be at least somewhat connected to your surroundings.

Augmented Reality Games and the Experience of Place

It's also interesting how AR gaming differs from what came before it. A history of gaming is beyond the scope of this book, but even glimpsing at some of the dominant trends in the industry shows a progression that centers increasingly on the experience of immersion in place. From the top-down view of Pac-Man and the side-scrolling view of Mario Bros., first-person perspective games like Doom and Halo have emerged. These latter games create an expectation of being immersed in the game's world, which increasingly feature rich textured landscapes.

And with augmented games, as opposed to a static escapist experience, we are offered an even more immersive experience that integrates our natural environment into a built partially artificial reality.

Connected Experiences . . . and Your Business Strategy?

This is only the beginning of what's to come.

People have been laughing at the businesses who are developing *Pokémon GO* strategies, but honestly, even they are a little late to the opportunity. The gold rush happened during the first two weeks, even if the game's popularity continues to grow. And if your business is still laughing, you're missing out on time to think about how augmented reality and connected experiences stand to change the status quo.

I'm not saying to rush out and do something specific to *Pokémon GO* that has no alignment with your customers' motivations or your brand. This is a call for strategic action about a macro trend, not mindless reaction to a micro trend. Trying to capitalize on the trend without strategy will probably come across as an attempt to manipulate the moment, but there's enough transformation taking place that there will be a relevant, meaningful way to make these opportunities align with your brand and your customers. Your job is to try to catch it.

Augmented Reality Shopping Experiences

We're used to the idea of being able to shop from home, from work, or from just about anywhere—e-commerce has been around in some form or other since the midnineties—but we're also used to the idea that shopping online means certain trade-offs. In exchange for the convenience of not having to go out, we accept that we won't have the benefit of sensory certainty, of being able to touch items, try them on, or consider them at scale alongside other items.

But with augmented reality shopping experiences, retailers have huge opportunities, in a range of contexts, to empower the shopper with contextual experiences that are as good or nearly as good as in-person. For the shopper, from the comfort of a home environment, we can, say, use a smartphone app to visualize a piece of furniture in the living room. The sensory experience may still excel in the dedicated retail environment of the store, but the trade-offs are changing.

Virtual Reality and Stories of Place

Society feels increasingly divided, increasingly fractured. There needs to be a way to overcome our differences.

Part of the problem, it seems, is that we have trouble empathizing when we haven't experienced something. This is where virtual reality presents an interesting advantage. Virtual reality presents compelling options for journalism and storytelling. In fact, one of the most promising ways we can use technology for social justice is through the use of virtual reality.

Virtual reality is a powerful tool for fostering empathy. Consider Chris Milk, who gave a compelling example in his TED talk[40]. He made the interactive video for Arcade Fire called "The Wilderness Downtown," which prompted viewers for their childhood address and then showed an array of video windows overlaid against one another. In the video a young man runs through streets, as images are pulled from Google Maps Street View of the area and ultimately the house that matches the address each viewer entered. It was effective, genius even, and it began to demonstrate the innovative opportunities of storytelling in a format that uses the ideas of home and place interactively to achieve resonance.

Later in his talk, Milk reveals a film of a twelve-year-old Syrian girl named Sidra, who's living in a refugee camp in Jordan. A photo or video of a girl in a refugee camp would certainly be enough to generate compassion in some people, and the most empathetic people may even begin to have a sense of what she must be going through. But with an immersive 360-degree virtual reality view, the ability for people to observe her conditions and surroundings allows them to picture themselves there in an unprecedented way.

By observing her in *place*—as if we share her location—we can better connect with her *humanity*. But the place must come alive for us first.

Through similar techniques, researchers in Japan have been working to create a virtual reality experience that simulates a tsunami with the hope of educating people living in areas at risk. The goal is for them to learn know how to respond and have a better chance of survival. In other words, that effort could connect people with their own place in a more adaptive way.

A person wearing virtual reality goggles (or some other hardware as it evolves) can be immersed in at least two senses—sight and hearing—almost as if they're there. The sense of place is far more complete than with a fixed two-dimensional representation. As a result, the narrative possibilities are enormous and potentially transformative.

360-Degree Video

If you've ever been somewhere like the Grand Canyon or Niagara Falls and tried to take a snapshot to remember it by, you know the impossibility of trying to depict a large-scale place in a photograph. Even a video that pans the landscape can seem underwhelming. As a firsthand observer, you have the benefit of moving your head and looking around, maybe looking back and forth and up and down, as your brain tries to process the information it's taking in.

Enter 360-degree video. It's a fully surrounded video shot with a specialized omnidirectional camera or with several cameras capturing footage in all directions simultaneously. When viewing, you can control the direction in view by moving to pan and scroll. If you're wearing goggles or headgear, you can spin around to see the imagery as if it is around you. It's visually immersive. (Many 360-degree videos are shot with surround sound, too, so the immersion can extend to the audio as well.)

In March 2015, YouTube began supporting 360-degree videos—after all, Google owns YouTube, and with YouTube support, Google's Cardboard headset viewer would become a fine way to experience them. So would an Oculus headset, and since Facebook owns Oculus, Facebook launched support for them in September 2015.

Like many emerging technologies, the full usefulness of the format is still being discovered. One 360-degree video that became popular in January 2016 showed the persistent lights of Times Square during the Jonas blizzard that blanketed the mid-Atlantic and Northeastern United States in as much as three feet of snow. That kind of newsworthy event— something that almost has to be seen to be believed—is probably a natural fit for such an immersive video experience. And this is probably just the beginning.

Even Twitter announced support for 360-degree video in June 2016. In a way, this step proves the technology's relevance as a trend since Twitter, unlike Google/YouTube and Facebook, doesn't have a VR headset product to promote. But you can still view 360-degree videos on the Twitter platform, and by dragging the image or tilting your phone, you can control the display as the video plays. Here again, the video format and the platform make for an interesting pair, particularly since breaking news happens more and more often on Twitter. But even cleverly branded content may recommend itself here. At least, it may be worth a try.

As for creating them, some of the earliest 360 videos were created with GoPro cameras and a Freedom 360 camera rig, which allows for spherical 360 video capture. These rugged cameras developed a reputation among outdoors enthusiasts and extreme athletes for being able to capture a thrilling video as the wearer skied down a steep slope or jumped off a bike ramp. They grew in popularity as demand grew for greater interactivity and immersion in video.

It's hard to say if GoPros were partly responsible for the increase in appetite or if they simply met up with an already growing appetite in the marketplace.

On the higher end of the capture experience, there are dedicated cameras and rigs, such as Giroptic, and you can certainly expect more to enter the market. On the lower end of capture, you can simply take a panoramic photo with your phone's camera; and if you post it to Facebook, it will show up within a 360-degree viewer.

This medium is full of exciting opportunities, and the stories you can tell are rich and compelling. The ability to communicate the experience of a place through digital channels keeps getting easier.

Camera Drones: "Augmented" Perspective

While not directly related to augmented reality or virtual reality, drones are an interesting aside and footnote to this discussion because they offer a sort of augmented take on the experience of a place that can alter how we perceive the place. While they used to be priced out of range for most private individuals, their prices have decreased. More of them have taken to the skies, capturing stunning aerial photography of cityscapes, fireworks, landmarks, and more.

The potential is high for interesting metadata, too: Every photo created by a digital camera produces a set of attributes as output known as the EXIF (Exchangeable Image File) data, such as exposure, flash, and more. Drone photo output has the potential to capture not only these image attributes but also embedded information about location, relative position, and so on; and a variety of aftermarket software solutions offer this. In this way, drones can produce a data stream to describe a perspective of place that could have creative and helpful uses in the future.

Overall, a drone is just another way to experience place. In a simplistic example, you could stand on a rooftop and use your phone's camera to take a photo, or you could fly a drone to capture the skyline view.

Whereas augmented reality experiences can involve the use of a camera to create a virtual layer "over top," figuratively speaking, of your physical surroundings, a drone is the use of a camera to create an augmented (or altered) perspective of your physical surroundings, often from literally "over top" of those surroundings. Moreover, not only is the output different because of its vantage point, but how you experience the capture of the moment differs, too.

CHAPTER TEN

Algorithms and AI

The category of developments that has both facilitated a great deal of the convergence of online and offline and where a huge amount of opportunity still has to play out is algorithms and AI. Strictly speaking, these two concepts don't necessarily belong in the same category, but I'm grouping them because today's algorithms influence tomorrow's artificial intelligence, and those together shape human experience.

So even beyond the consideration of experience taking place in physical space or digital, and beyond the convergence of these layers, when we're talking about human experience at all anymore, we have to understand that more and more of it relies on algorithms and AI and the rich data model that underpins everything.

Since part of our exploration in this book is into the metaphors that describe experience, it's of interest to note that there are a whole set of metaphors in the field of AI that anthropomorphize machines, such as machine "learning." And of course "intelligence."

Human Bias

Algorithms are just sets of rules. For now, until machines develop their own algorithms, we are the ones who determine those rules. I hope it is easy to see where there's a path from quietly holding our own biases to unintentionally encoding machines with them.

Here's the other tricky part: Artificial intelligence has to start somewhere, with some set of rules, some set of givens.

What we are then asking machines to do is process the world and learn about it from a starting point that, by some necessity, includes our own hidden intentions and prejudices.

Because it has to, at some level. When you deconstruct far enough, you can see how simply presenting world maps as north-is-up and south-is-down carries some bias. How the common phrasing of "his and hers" or "he and she" carries bias, as the male pronoun by default comes first. How black=dark=bad or evil, and white=light=pure or good. There are plenty of cultural assumptions that are widespread and nearly universal —the legacy flaws in our own human programming. That we build data models that contain these biases is a shame; that we risk passing these biases over to learning machines is nearly tragic.

Yet it happens all the time, and some of the inherited biases produce results with relatively minor consequences, such as the movie ratings on Fandango.com skewing higher than those elsewhere, as discussed in the earlier section, "Fair Isn't Always Fair." But some of the results have consequences with real financial costs, or even costs to social justice and equality. Fresno police mine social media to assign residents a "threat score."[41] Researchers at Carnegie Mellon University found that women weren't seeing ads for higher-paying jobs as often as men on Google's ad network.[42] Analysis of Uber wait times in D.C. showed longer waits in neighborhoods with more people of color.

It's clear that algorithms and the platforms they power can have some inherently unfair design tics. We have to be aware of bias and privilege when we think about machine learning, because we need to recognize what we're teaching machines to learn. We also have to be careful what we ask technology to do for us, or we risk encoding nuances of hidden intention and bias in the machines we ask to go on learning from that framework.

All in all, if we're designing experiences, we're accountable for how we model fairness in the data we collect through human interactions, as well as how the algorithms we build make decisions against that human data.

Filter Bubble

In 2011, Eli Pariser hit a nerve with his TED Talk and the book it drew from, *The Filter Bubble: What the Internet Is Hiding from You.* The upshot?

That personalization algorithms for online content are shaping what we consume (and to some extent, what we are able to consume) so that we are less and less exposed to divergent ideas.[13]

Pariser's talk cites how Netflix, among other commerce examples, applies personalization. That's what got me thinking about how this algorithmic content evolution relates to online marketing, e-commerce, and our ethical responsibilities as marketers. Oddly, even though many of my friends who shared this video are themselves thinkers about digital marketing and online social sharing, there seems to be very little introspection about what the "filter bubble" effect means in terms of online marketing and ethics.

In my digital analytics agency, we encouraged our e-commerce clients to test behavioral targeting. There's typically a great deal of convenience that this kind of targeting affords the customer. For example, Amazon knows that I tend to buy vegan cookbooks, so it tends to show me the latest and best-rated related books in my browse path. I welcome this because I get exposed to books I somehow might have missed but will almost certainly like. If I were in a bookstore, these might be shelved together anyway, but metadata and personalization can help make those recommendations even better. On Netflix, too, there's a good chance that showing me personalized suggestions will save me time and delight me, even as it reinforces my longevity with the site and ensures my subscription payments for months to come.

This selfish/selfless balance is the new normal in marketing optimization. It's what I personally am passionate about: using data to create better customer experiences and, simultaneously, generate incremental profits. It's what we do with our clients, and their KPIs speak for themselves.

But are we contributing to this insular and narcissistic phenomenon where the more time individuals spend online, the more mirrors are set up around them so that they can no longer see diverse behavior, but rather increasingly similar likenesses of themselves? Perhaps. After all, one of the keys to the work we do is an emphasis on relevance. As I think of it, relevance is a form of respect. It shows customers that we respect their time and effort enough not to make them scour the site for what they're after.

Chris Brogan and other digital thought leaders have spoken about social news as a serendipity engine. (*Serendipity*, incidentally, has long been my favorite word and a beloved concept.) In earlier iterations of social news, you got what you got. So, too, in early e-commerce. As the availability of information has accelerated, though, and personalization algorithms have evolved, some of that serendipity has been traded for distillation and, yes, relevance. So, sure, from an editorial perspective, in the video Pariser is justified in saying that Mark Zuckerberg's example of "a squirrel dying in front of your house" is not as important as "people dying in Africa." But in commerce, the dilemma of moral or ethical priority is not nearly so clear-cut. Perhaps the personalization of search and social news makes it less likely that you'll happen upon something random and wonderful, but the continued explosion of long-tail content and commerce means there's randomness even within niches. While the "filter bubbles" Pariser describes might obscure your view of the randomness and chaos of the web, in general, personalization does help uncover hidden gems within customers' interests.

Because the other side of all this tailoring and customization is that the long tail is getting longer in every area, and the realization that we're not going to be able to see most of what's out there is starting to sink in. So personalized content and merchandising is as much a response to information overload as it is to data availability. Going back to my earlier example, if I landed on Amazon's home page and it made no effort to customize the content for me, it's likely I'd have little idea of the breadth and depth of its catalog as it related to the semi-obscure offerings that appeal to me. Would I think to search for chia seeds, one of my recent purchases at the site, if it hadn't been made clear to me that Amazon carried food as well as books (and tools and shoes and sporting equipment . . . and, and, and)?

After all, relevance and targeting are not new phenomena in marketing. We study demographic and psychographic information to understand customer profiles so that we can tailor our advertising placements, our message, and our follow-through for optimal results. What's newer is the ability to adjust whole experiences on the fly based on behavioral performance. Imagine if you walked into a store—let's use Nordstrom as an example, since it's famous for its quality concierge service. As you looked around and your attention landed on an object, the other objects around you shifted. Would you feel more catered to or more pandered to? Or perhaps both? In the context of Nordstrom, where it has been established that it's trying to improve your shopping experience, perhaps it would only seem like another level of superior customer service. If you had the same experience in, say, Walmart, chances are a savvy shopper might feel manipulated.

As a marketer, I see my job as creating meaningful connections between company and customer. (Note that I don't say that my job is to convert customers: I'm an advocate of empathy-oriented optimization as opposed to conversion. The latter as a single KPI is too narrow and shortsighted.) As a data-driven, technology-savvy marketer, I know that behavioral similarities among visitors, and ultimately customers, often lead to clues, validated through analysis and testing, that can improve the customer experience overall—and, in turn, increase profit. That this also occasionally means limiting a customer's view of the site and creating an insulated experience is not only an acceptable side effect, it's intentional. That's what customer behavior dictates. Customers become overwhelmed when presented with too much choice, and since niche options abound online, that means that if I'm HomeDepot.com and a customer comes in from a search for power tools, I'd best show top-selling power tools and not home appliances or ladders.

Perhaps a lesson to take away is that there might be opportunity in exposing the customer experience to a little randomness, as long as it doesn't interfere with the customers' intentions. A little unexpected cross-sell of something charming, a quirky-but-fun site feature, something surprising and fresh—these types of experiments with commercial randomness might be worth trying in your environment, to see how customers respond. Because with all of the filtering we're presented with, the savvy shoppers out there might be picking up on the sometimes heavy-handed crafting of custom-tailored experiences. And maybe, just maybe, we're all overdue for a little serendipity anyway.

The overemphasis on personalization just may be making serendipity more interesting. Showing a customer a little randomness alongside their personalized recommendations serves two purposes: First, it provides a little relief to the person seeing the recommendations, since they're so used to being creeped out by hyper-targeted content. Second, it offers the chance of a spark of inspiration: something the person may have meant to look up and forgot. And for you as a marketer, it serves as an interesting baseline. It's a control, and it can help you gauge how effective the personalization is.

It is often said that we are drowning in information. (We're drowning in misinformation, too.[44]) But I think we are adapting more quickly than we realize. We are developing increasingly sophisticated filters to tune out what we don't want to see, hear, or know. But why are we susceptible to being in a bubble? Precisely because we are not seeing the meaning of what we take in.

Humanlike Nuances

There are subtleties about being human and dealing with humans that we sometimes underestimate.

In the age of machine learning/artificial intelligence/cognitive computing, we have to ask what it means to be human, and what is uniquely human as opposed to a learnable response.

More and more often, machines are accomplishing feats of intelligence and reasoning once thought to be human-dominated, from winning a game of Go with its exhaustive possibilities that seem to rely on something like intuition to evaluate,[45] to extrapolating patterns from a single example[46], and more. There's something that's going on there that will definitely inform the way we richly experience our surrounding environments.

Empathy, for example, seems as if it would be one of those traits, but there are examples of AI being taught to show empathy, or at least make decisions on factors that resemble intuition and human insight. A machine-learning algorithm has been able to identify tweets sent under the influence of alcohol.[47] Google has been feeding romance novels to its artificial intelligence engine to give it a framework for the nuances of emotion and empathy, in hopes that this will make it more conversational.[48]

Logical analysis has limits. We rely on complex systems of intuition, empathy, and insight in making ethical choices, and passing these burdens to artificial intelligence doesn't yet seem possible[49]. But that doesn't mean it won't happen, and it doesn't mean there aren't developments meanwhile using humanlike interactions in technology that can aid our human experience.

For example, someone built an app that gives computer-generated directions the way a human would.[50] Or might.

Image via Walc

Walc is an app that uses nearby landmarks to orient the user throughout the directions. Take a left after the Apple Store, walk towards Macy's, and so on.

It's not necessarily context-aware, but the app was built with an awareness of the context a human might be in when needing directions —navigating through an unfamiliar part of town, or looking for cues that they're on the right track.

The evolution of integrated experiences will inevitably involve algorithms and artificial intelligence, but there's still something to be said for weaving in those qualities we consider to be uniquely human, even as some of those characteristics become less unique to us.

The Guided Experience Economy: Artificial Experience and

Conversational Commerce

There's a lot of talk about the "experience economy," and I do think experiences are going to be increasingly important to design for—hence, this book—but I think there's a more interesting facet of this overall economy that gets at something more transformative.

If you combine the notion of the experience economy with what we're seeing of conversational commerce, then you end up with something a little more like these:

- Voice
- Bots
- Chat
- Social

Some, like Sarah Guo of Greylock Partners, are calling this combination the "conversational economy." As she wrote in *VentureBeat*, the term *conversational economy* encompasses the growth of:

1) messaging applications, 2) voice-controlled computing, 3) bots and services that sit—or just start—within messaging apps / voice-controlled hardware, and 4) enabling, picks-and-shovels products.[51]

Yet the point isn't so much the conversation. After all, very few people are excited about having conversations with computers. Instead, what it really speaks to (if you'll pardon the pun) is the richness and agility of the guidance that can be offered through these interfaces. So I'm calling it the "guided experience economy." As these lightweight and adaptable forms of interaction develop into mainstream usage, we will see some very interesting opportunities across industries for how the guided experience economy can play out both online and offline.

Icelandair is providing a very helpful proof of concept of what the guided experience economy looks like in practice offline. PSFK.com reported that for a limited time, "Those embarking on an Icelandair Stopover can request the complimentary companionship of an Icelandair employee, who then serves as a field and cultural guide to the wintry wonderland."

That facet of experience economy, offering some physical service that augments the experience of a place, is a placemaking interpretation. But the opportunities are enormous when those placemaking instincts are aided by technology.

For example, what if you could combine that idea with autonomous/

driverless cars and AI developed to personalize recommendations for traveler preferences? You end up with a very interesting beginning to a whole new macro platform that goes beyond delivery services and into AI-guided tourism and more.

You also end up with some very useful adaptability. During college, when I was a German major, I picked up a job giving German-language guided tours of Chicago. One Saturday morning, I stood in the lobby of the hotel where I was to meet my guests and held up my tour guide sign. It didn't take long to realize that this particular group was actually Greek, not German. It was probably a simple data entry error on the part of whoever at my employer company took the order—after all, German and Greek were most likely directly next to each other in the list of languages on some tour order database screen. But with my employer's office closed on Saturdays, it was too late to swap out tour guides; and although no one in the group spoke English, one happened to speak German. So I gave the tour in German, and he translated, and we all had a great time.

It's a fun story to be able to tell, although not all such stories would have charming outcomes. Perhaps an intelligent assistant, with the ability to deliver information in a variety of languages on a self-driving tour bus, would improve the guests' experience. Although perhaps it ended up being surprisingly more fun than if the tour guide had been correctly assigned.

It's also a delightful example of how the story of technology's role in human life is so often about being helpful until it's spectacularly and wildly unhelpful. Perhaps our role as designers of experience is to anticipate as much as we can of the process so we can alleviate as much unhelpfulness as possible.

***

As some designers have been saying, the new UI is no UI. Or it's at least a user interface that differs significantly from the windows-based screen interfaces we spent most of the '80s, '90s, and 2000s thinking of as "computers." Although touch, gesture, and haptic feedback in general have been around in various forms for decades (who had one of those vibrating game joysticks back in the day?), their uses are becoming far more common since the popularization of touch screen devices like the iPhone.

That's all part of the shift, but aside from the evolution toward touch-based and haptic interfaces (especially in VR), voice is natural and faster than other modes of interaction and navigation for everyday needs. Voice-based devices like Amazon Echo and Google Home are the beginning of what is likely to be a wave of adaptive assistants for home and beyond in the coming years. And chat-based interactions are mobile-friendly and well suited to user conditions where voice might be a more socially challenging means of interacting.

Now what to do with all of that in placemaking?

An app-driven experience in a place that people visit only rarely, like a museum, a zoo, or a ballpark, can be cumbersome to initiate. These places often rely on QR codes that link the visitor to a download of the app, and then the visitor has to fumble through remembering their device password, setting up an account, and so on.

* * *

Photos I took at the Irish Hunger Memorial

As a straightforward example, here's an opportunity I encountered recently where conversational interaction, or something other than a QR code leading to an app, could have been useful. I happened upon the Irish Hunger Memorial while walking through New York City's Battery Park City area, and since the Irish famine was part of my ancestry's experience, I wanted to find out more about the memorial and the famine it commemorates. Attached to the wall of the memorial was a laminated sign that offered a downloadable app, complete with QR code linking to the download.

There were several problems with this: One, I'd deleted the QR code reader app off of my phone some time ago due to lack of use and lack of relevance, so I didn't have the wherewithal to first download a reader, then scan, download, and set up a dedicated museum app. Most visitors to moments, memorials, and even museums are just not going to do it. Asking visitors to download a dedicated app is not a proportional level of involvement and commitment for what is most likely going to be a one-time visit. Secondly, I didn't have a very strong cell signal, and my battery was getting low; so doing all that downloading would have been too resource-intensive for my circumstances.

On the other hand, a chat-based interface would have been ideal. The sign could have offered a short code visitors could text to initiate, with prompts to receive more information. Even directing me to social media accounts where perhaps there might be some explanatory multimedia would have been helpful and less resource-intensive than downloading an app (or two apps, in situations like mine). And that might have earned the accounts an ongoing follower. (For more on museum opportunities, see "Museums and Interpretation: Holding Space for an Idea.")

For retailers, it's abundantly clear. (See "Retail: Transcending the Transactional and Creating Value Beyond the Purchase" for more on this.) But for other industries, it might take a little more creativity. How will museums make use of conversational chatbots? How might healthcare make use of voice assistants? We're already seeing an inkling of the answer: Amazon Echo can now give light medical assistance in diagnosing symptoms. "Alexa, I have a headache. What should I do?" "Do you have a fever?" "No." "Take aspirin." That may not be exactly how that conversation goes, but it's the gist. And other industries will follow suit.

CHAPTER ELEVEN

Considerations for Meaningful Human Experience Design

When you're dealing with a topic that's changing every single day, it's a challenge to write a book in a way that will allow it to remain relevant for years to come. But there are elements that are common to the design of meaningful human experiences that I've observed and validated over years with a wide variety of clients, and these elements are timeless. So this next section takes a step back from looking at specific examples of technologies and implementations to look instead at some frameworks and tools that can help you and your organization design more meaningful experiences that integrate and transcend physical and digital surroundings.

Some of the key elements of meaningful human experience design are:

- Intentionality (which you could also call Purpose)
- Dimensionality
- Metaphors and Cognitive Associations
- Value and Emotional Load
- Alignment and Effectiveness
- Adaptation and Iteration

These elements really come to life when considered alongside the process for cultivating meaning in experience overall. I have developed what I call the Meaningfulness Model to help experience-makers of all kinds (marketers, entrepreneurs, placemakers, etc.) achieve greater meaning through strategy and design.

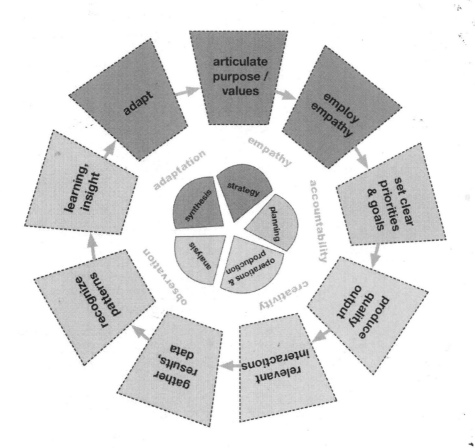

meaningfulness model

The Meaningfulness Model is intended to be iterative, as the arrows suggest. Loosely, you'd start in the top center, with purpose, and work your way around. It's never that simple or neat, though, because insights often show up announced, out of sequence; and real life doesn't always stick to the plan. That's okay—it can still be helpful as a directional tool, as a guide for making good decisions and moving toward greater insights and greater success.

As you go through the process of experimenting and learning what helps you fulfill your objectives and what doesn't, what resonates with customers and what doesn't, what keeps visitors coming back and what doesn't, and so on, you can adapt the technologies you put into place to integrate physical and digital experience in more and more meaningful ways.

In the next sections, I'll look more closely at intentionality, dimensionality, semantic layer and literal messaging, metaphors and cognitive associations, and emotional load. These elements, particularly when explored through an iterative learning approach like the Meaningfulness Model, will help focus your efforts toward achieving memorable and meaningful experiences that integrate the realities of physical surroundings and available technology in seamless ways.

Intentionality, or Purpose

One of the key ingredients in meaning-making is purpose, and because we know this, it stands to reason that one of the foundational elements in the Meaningful Human Experience Design framework must be related to purpose. But I like to call this "intentionality" because this element is not only about having a clear sense of what we want to do or what we hope to achieve, but also about the framing that we're going to be *intentional* each step of the way in achieving that outcome.

Even in my strategy workshops, I usually start by asking clients to spend just a few minutes working with me to formulate a statement that encompasses the objective for the day, for the project, or for the campaign. Sometimes that takes the shape of something like: "Define strategy and develop a testing roadmap for the launch of the XYZ product," or "Identify relevant messages to use in sales calls with different stakeholders."

In other words, what would success look like? We're setting our intention, and that helps keep the meeting on track. That also leads to clarity around whether what we're discussing now is getting us there. Discussions that might have seemed off-topic can sometimes lead to uncovering roadblocks to the outcomes.

However you approach this in your environment for your projects, it's just important that you do it. You might call it purpose; you might just call it strategy. You could do this as a task force or as an individual. You don't need to stick to any sort of script. What matters is that each time we set out to design the experiences that human beings are going to have with our ideas, our brands, and our places, we are giving honest and thoughtful consideration to the dynamics that are at work or will be at work in the bigger picture and are trying to articulate how we hope to influence the outcome.

Thinking about the role of place in experience design presupposes some purpose anyway; a bathroom and a kitchen have quite different human experience design considerations.

Also, the human experience of the place is bound to have some sense of stillness within it or movement through it, as discussed in the earlier section, "Movement Versus Stillness." I either want to be there or I don't, and if I don't want to be there (such as in a hospital), I need to sense that you empathize with that. I want to feel you've designed my experience to be as easy and as painless as possible. That goes into the journey mapping (also discussed earlier in "Maps: Mapping Physical Place Versus Maps of Experience: Empathy Maps, Journey Maps"), the considerations of process and progress and flow and movement through.

You can design that awareness into the physical elements of the hospital building itself, into the training given to the receptionist, into the website, into the wayfinding signage. But it also goes into the technology considerations, such as whether to use an electronic medical records system that provides patient access to test results and a simple appointment scheduling interface. It goes into the data management decisions that pertain to security and file storage. It goes into the policies that protect the patient data, and when it is done well, it goes into the culture of the hospital staff, too. It goes everywhere, because purpose is at its best when it is more than a mission statement; it is at its best when it provides the foundation for the whole operation. (Operation! No pun intended.)

There has to be some awareness of purpose in experience design to be able to employ appropriate technology. Otherwise, it's too easy to get caught up in what's trendy. You cannot force a solution onto a problem you haven't taken the time to define, and the result is bound to feel clunky. (See my example in "The Guided Experience Economy: Artificial Experience and Conversational Commerce.")

Priorities

One of the stages in the Meaningfulness Model is "setting clear priorities and goals." In terms of meaning-making overall, that effort lends itself toward accountability within the process, so that we're honest with ourselves about what works and what doesn't. In a related way, it's also a component of meaningful human experience design. It's key to know what the priorities of the system are.

One of the interpretations of meaning, you may recall from "Meaning, and Why It Matters Here," is that it's about what matters. Priorities put what matters front and center.

Integrated experiences can become cluttered and crowded with unnecessary prompts for interaction and unnecessary promotions. And the efforts to gather insights can become bogged down by unnecessary data collection.

So it's important to determine what matters, to set priorities for the interfaces, to set priorities for the marketing, to set priorities through the business operations, and to streamline around those priorities. The experiences will be better for it, and your organization will operate in greater alignment with your priorities and goals.

Relevance to Person, Relevance to Purpose

I often say, "Relevance is a form of respect." (I usually add: "And so is discretion.") People generally appreciate being shown that you've tried to consider their priorities and context (within reason, hence the addendum about discretion). The experiences you design have to be relevant both to your brand's purpose and relevant to the person with whom you're interacting.

To design for human experience, we have to be conscious of context and align the messages and experiences with what is likely to be relevant to someone's interests and motivations and needs at that moment.

I want to emphasize that true consideration for their needs and where they are in their life journey is the foundational work here, but extending from this, it can be helpful to think about incentives that strengthen their interest in spending time, money, and attention on you. You might consider, say, gamification elements, especially if you're developing an experience around a system with complexity. You might reward people for engaging with your brand in a way that builds their comfort with the system and provides you with data about their usage so that you can fine-tune accordingly. LinkedIn did this well in their early days. They wanted people to fill out their profiles, which would strengthen other people's interest in the platform; so they displayed a percentage score on the user interface showing how complete a profile was. If you'd added your current job and title, but hadn't filled in previous employment history or education, your score (visible only to you) might say 60 percent. If you did everything but add a profile picture, it might say 90 percent. And that last 10 percent could nag just enough for a lot of users to go ahead and add the picture, just to complete the 100 percent.

Loyalty programs often involve a form of this incentive, and with physical-digital integration, you can reward people with whatever they will value—whether that's a discount, visibility, or whatever it may be—for things like checking into the store on Foursquare or Facebook, posting a picture on Instagram, posting a snap on Snapchat with your geo-filter, etc.

The right approach will vary from context to context; it will depend on your intended outcome—your purpose—from which you can determine priorities. With a better understanding of purpose, it will be easier to accomplish what is relevant both for you and for the people with whom you're interacting.

Dimensionality

See if you can call to mind a few of the most memorable and meaningful major experiences in your life. I don't know about you, but for me, these experiences—life changes, decisions, moments of realization, moments of impact—all have a sense of popping out of the timeline, transcending the space where they occurred, having heightened connectedness with other people, with community, with myself.

That's what meaningful experiences do. They transcend dimensions and appear larger than life.

Meaningful experiences transcend dimensions and appear larger than life.

So when we are in the role of designing human experience, and we aim to create meaningful and memorable interactions, we need to have some awareness of how they'll weave into the tapestry of the authentic life moments our counterparts are having on the other side of the designed experience. Most marketers, designers, and strategists are probably not working in a domain that will lend itself to a major life-changing memory for their users and customers, but some are; and the experiences any of us create could easily be the backdrop against which major life moments play out. Someone could be having the best or worst day of their lives when they come into contact with our store, website, app, etc. Having some empathy for that possibility allows us to consider the layers of context that may overwhelm seemingly simple interactions.

In addition, of course, when you're planning integrated physical and digital experiences, there's a good deal more layered realities to keep up with. What's powerful about these is that you have a data layer describing them, so the metadata of the experience itself opens dimensional connections with other people throughout time and space who have shared this experience. For example, when a person posts a picture to Instagram of the Brooklyn Bridge, if they use the location tag and select "Brooklyn Bridge," or add the hashtag "#brooklynbridge" or a related hashtag, they then have the opportunity to click through to the stream of people who have also shared pictures with those tags, and interact with them along that shared dimension. This can become even more meaningful when the place has deep significance for them, and they can see how the place is significant for other people, too.

Whether you're designing an app like Instagram or you're the person responsible for the Brooklyn Bridge's digital presence or public relations, this meaning and metadata dimensionality can help you think in a more sophisticated way about the interests of the people who are your users and visitors; and you can better influence what tools and content you make available.

You might see value in thinking of these layers the way urban planners do site analysis, in cutaways that reveal the elements contributing to the overall experience.

Image source: An Camas Mór

The image above shows a diagram from a community project in Scotland designed by Gehl Architects. As I've mentioned, the Danish architect Jan Gehl has been one of the key voices on human-centered city life in the last few decades. This approach to planning shows how people and the human experience can come first, with the built environment then being designed around human needs and public life.

The layers you consider in integrating physical and digital experiences may include more conceptual, more abstract, and perhaps more subjective ideas for example, values, capabilities, and so on, as well as elements that are demonstrable and objective, such as proximity and time or frequency.

Even thinking about a website experience with cutaway layers reveals the opportunity to design for dimensionality, to make sure that the needs of varying users can be met

Meaningful Human Experience Design: Site Analysis Framework

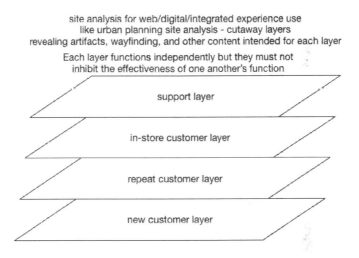

site analysis for web/digital/integrated experience use
like urban planning site analysis - cutaway layers
revealing artifacts, wayfinding, and other content intended for each layer

Each layer functions independently but they must not
inhibit the effectiveness of one another's function

support layer

in-store customer layer

repeat customer layer

new customer layer

Then the study of dimensionality comes back to metaphor, and movement. What is the metaphor for the progress of your users or constituents through their journey? Are they moving through time? Does their history in some way figure into their current experience? Are they learning, as in a graduation?

How will you connect them to their present surroundings, while in a sense freeing them of those surroundings at the same time?

Value and Emotional Load
* * *

133

In the most primitive form of business, I am a baker and you are a carpenter. You need my bread to eat, and I need the furniture you build to prepare bread and eat it on. We can barter, but one loaf of bread will probably not have the same value as one table. So we can trade unequal amounts to establish a placeholder of relative value. Within a few trades, we will probably have established currency. (But not Bitcoin, yet.)

Either way, in determining the value of the goods, we assess their meaning to us. We consider our need of them. We assess their quality—the craftsmanship that went into the baking of the bread or the building of the table—and we ascribe meaning to that time and skill. We note the aesthetics: the sensory experiences of the bread, the quality of the ingredients. The shaping of the table legs, the strength of the joints. Maybe we are reminded of the aroma of freshly baked bread in our grandmother's kitchen. We remember the worn old table she leaned over, dusting it with flour, kneading the dough.

The meaning is emotional and unintentional. It is intrinsic. We are not purely objective; we cannot distance ourselves from our experiences.

Value in business is inseparable from meaning, yet we often talk about value as if it were simply a price point—as if you can take the jumbled landscape of sense memories, beauty, irrational fears, prized beliefs, aspirations, accomplishments, and everything else, roll it into a snowball of whatever size, and call it "price." Only to watch it melt.

Meaning does not melt or shrink; meaning grows. When you start from an understanding of meaning, you can operate on wholly different dimensions. You can assess the value of a thing to someone based on what you understand of their desires. Based on they want and need, based on what they cherish, based on what they will fight for, walk away from, laugh at, cry at, share with strangers, and hide from friends. You can begin to see opportunities to add value to a thing based on how you deliver it, where you make it available, when you communicate about it, what you add to it, what you leave out, what color you make it, what you call it, etc.

This is also where it helps to recognize an underlying idea that frames the interactions and transactions, such as Third Place for Starbucks, or how Southwest lets its passengers share in their playful quest for operational efficiencies. (As discussed in the earlier section on "Starbucks, "Third Place," and the Power of Strategic Framing.") This is using meaning in its most powerful way: to align what matters and achieve greater resonance and a sense of truth among everyone involved.

Integrated physical and digital experiences have incredible potential for this kind of intentional design around value. People bring so many layered associations into how they interact in a given place: sense memories, cultural and subcultural interpretations, family history, their personal narrative and aspirational self, the context of their present circumstances, and so on. As you anticipate the evolution of their relationship with you, the journey through stages and touchpoints, the life cycle of their role as your customer or patient or student, it can be vividly clarifying to think about what they value so that you can align your objectives with theirs.

Achieving meaning is holistically both reactive and predictive. If I listen closely to what you tell me, I can adjust what I offer you accordingly. In the primitive transaction, this was a manual and physical process, both verbal and nonverbal. Today, digital listening is both possible and necessary. And with integrated physical and digital experiences, if the data model allows it, that "digital listening" has a lot to say about movement through place, too, and it all ties back together to enrich the understanding of what's meaningful. Every opportunity to hear—deeply hear—what someone communicates about what they value, however they communicate it as it relates to our offering, is an invitation to create meaning together.

If we listen, people constantly tell us what they value. It's not the free shipping that a person values; it's often something a level higher and more intrinsic, like the freedom and delight they feel because now that extra errand there was no time for isn't necessary. People don't value curtains, per se; they value that the curtains make their homes feel cozier, more complete, and sometimes a little more private.

Listening gives us the data to understand meaning and value, and empathy gives us the ability to make something with it. We have the opportunity to create meaningful relationships between our businesses and our customers with every interaction. The more you try to understand what your product means to your customer, the more you can build upon its value.

Emotional Load

In addition to emotional associations that comprise the value people assign to certain interactions, some types of interactions between customer and business take place when the customer is amid some sort of crisis or distress. These distress purchases are often driven by different priorities in the decision-making process. Price, for example, may still be an important consideration in such a moment, but the evaluation of price may be at a cursory comparative level—just making sure they're not getting overcharged before they opt for your service. Whatever the specifics of the shift as it plays out in your marketplace and with the prospective customers for your business, people make different decisions when in distress. They are carrying an emotional load.

When you plan and design for a meaningful experience, you have to know what kind of emotional load a customer is likely carrying. It will color the experience from the beginning on their end, which means you need to anticipate it at the beginning of the interaction.

There must be an understanding of what value is created or exchanged in the designing of the place for humans. In retail, the value is usually something to do with ease and perhaps enjoyment of the purchase process itself; in hospitals, the value is generally security and reassurance that you or your loved one is in good hands and will be better soon.

Designing for integrated experiences means being aware of the ways in which physical space can interact with the emotional load they're already carrying. Hospitals can often be big and daunting and impersonal, and considering how many people walking through the front doors are there under some kind of distressing circumstances—due to their own medical condition or that of someone they love—the already overwhelming experience is amplified.

Technology and connected experiences can't solve all the problems related to this, but done well, they can be a start. If a hospital were to conceptualize the experience as an empowering one rather than an overwhelming one, they could work through all the ways they would need to put power in the hands of the patient and visitor in order to fulfill that idea. How might wayfinding be different? How might, dare I say, billing be different? How the organization interacts with the human can be built out through the integrated experience in some way, and the more aligned the components are, the more successful the experience will be.

Metaphors and Cognitive Associations

If the earlier chapter on metaphors ("Chapter Eight - Metaphors: Digital Experience Through the Lens of Place") hasn't made the point already, allow me to be clear: Using the right metaphors can be a key part of success.

What cognitive associations are users and constituents likely to have about the brand, the process, and/or the experience?

The framework of metaphors and cognitive associations exist in a layer of abstraction that isn't usually exposed directly. But the experience will also have a semantic or communication layer, where the messaging occurs, and you convey the ideas underlying the system to the user of the system. The semantic layer is where the metaphor rubber meets the messaging road. There's always some kind of communication layer, even if it's nonverbal/nonwritten. (Think of IKEA's assembly instructions, done entirely in cartoonish diagrams, which saves them having to provide translations.) Even integrated physical-digital experiences have communication layers, some of which may happen through a digital device and some of which may happen in the physical surroundings through signage, wayfinding design, aesthetics, the arrangement of elements in the space, etc. In any case, these formative ideas of metaphor and cognitive associations need at least one more layer to communicate well with people experiencing them, which is usually where narrative and story come in.

Narrative and Story

How do you weave metaphor and cognitive associations into *both* your understanding of the user's experience *and* the user's understanding of the intended experience? Metaphorical associations are codified through visual cues, such as the overused magnifying glass to represent "Search." But another layer of that communication happens through narrative, and this brings with it the opportunity to develop a history—of the story created by the place, of the user's experience of the place—and to connect the metaphors the place brings with it in a cohesive way.

You can dig into this by asking some questions:

What story are you trying to tell with your interactions? What story is

137

the person using your product or service going through?

What kinds of narrative will you need to construct, and how will you measure the customer journey through that narrative?

How can you reinforce that narrative regardless of context?

Story has a natural place in thinking about metaphor and cognitive associations, but it's also another way of dimensionalizing the experience for the people who engage with your brand, service, product, or place. There are many books and guides that have explored the components of story in great detail, so I won't attempt to reproduce that knowledge here; but by using the classic elements of story (such as hero, goal, conflict, and so on), you have a chance at humanizing the brand for the user and humanizing the user for the brand.

Alignment and Effectiveness

In order to create meaningful or memorable experiences, there has to be a sense of alignment between the entity that governs a physical or digital space and the humans who use it, inhabit it, buy in it, and travel through it. This effort to align the needs and motives of the players involved emphasizes similarity and brings strength.

Alignment is important in business and strategy overall. It's important to align sales and marketing—reduces operating costs, marketing and technology, customer motives and company motives, etc.

As an aside, I think a lot of what falls into the term *growth hacking*—a term that sounds dishonest and manipulative—could just as easily be described as *alignment marketing*, where natural overlaps between the customer's interest and the company's interest are force multipliers of success.

There are also force multiples in strategic alignment of product development:

Many of the innovation of 3Ms like Post-it notes, magnetic tape, and photographic films are the results of leveraging its expertise in substrates, coatings and adhesives. RIMs success with Blackberry smart phone is based on designing its features around the company's strategic focus on enterprise business. RIM's recent innovation on Blackberry PlayBook is again based on its business-centric features.[52]

It's also important to align offline brand experience design with online brand experience design.

That's a lot of alignment to strive for. Trying to do it all at once can sometimes hold back well-intentioned efforts and allow misaligned campaigns and projects to go forward without consideration.

So just as it's important to treat the knowledge gathering process as iterative, it's important to treat alignment as an iterative process, too. You may need to be tactical and responsive before you can be strategic and proactive, but don't let the first stage keep you from getting to the next.

With strategic alignment, marketing organizations are able to develop measurement architectures or strategies that not only answer the question of "Was this tactic successful?" but also "How impactful was it to the overall business objectives?"[53]

A key question to ask is:

What are the motivations of the people using your space, and how do they or how can they align with your motivations for designing the space?

The more you can align these motivations, the more you can use technology and data to cement the relationship.

In assessing the capabilities of the organization and what opportunities you have, you might find it helpful to use a framework like this as a starting point for thinking through strategic alignment with your organization—beginning from capabilities, developing deeper data to validate, and refining through iterations over time:

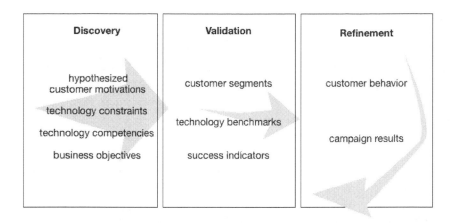

Discovery	Validation	Refinement
hypothesized customer motivations	customer segments	customer behavior
technology constraints	technology benchmarks	
technology competencies		campaign results
business objectives	success indicators	

You have to be willing to align internally and externally, to take results and knowledge from validation experiments and not only apply them to ongoing campaigns and external efforts, but also to gaps in talent. You can reorganize and strengthen the organization around what comes through learning.

Effectiveness

There has to be a sense of how to measure or otherwise gauge the effectiveness, or the success, of the designed experience in a physical or digital space. This is where you measure the success or at least clarify what isn't working. The more you can define up front what success will look like, the more you can use technology and data to measure whether you got there.

In my consulting, I often tell clients that the first time through a new marketing operations process is not necessarily about gaining big wins in conversion rate or revenue or anything like that. It's to familiarize everyone with the process; to identify who will be responsible for signing off on what; to decide who needs to get the line of Javascript inserted into the code, and so on. Once you get through that process, you can make adjustments as needed and do it again right away, becoming more effective each time you go through it.

Adaptation and Iteration

It happens every so often. I'm consulting with a client and we've worked our way through almost a whole strategic cycle, and then we get to the learnings. The results of our efforts show that the product might make more sense without a certain distracting feature, or that the website is hemorrhaging visitors and that the design is probably too unfocused. Or something. Whatever it is, something suggests that in order to make good on what we've learned, either the message or the product or the organization or *something* has to change.

Unfortunately, many organizations—from huge enterprises to small nonprofits—are led with a certain amount of resistance to change. Perhaps it's because the top leadership fears that change implies they've been leading in the wrong direction, or perhaps it's because change always sounds like it's going to be very expensive and chaotic, or perhaps it's another reason entirely.

But resistance to change is real and all too common.

Maybe you've tried out a beacon program and learned something about merchandising that changes what you thought you knew about your most popular products.

Maybe you used a location-targeted advertisement to test out a message and it worked so well you now think it might need to inform (and maybe replace) your overall marketing strategy.

It stands to reason that integrated experiences, as they pull in more data, are also poised to bring in more insights about what needs to change in the organization in order to make good on the data and insights

Organizations must have a certain amount of agility and openness to change.

Change sounds big and scary, though. I prefer to use the term *adaptation*.

Adaptation conjures up images of Darwin and evolution, and that's okay. (In the marketing world, it has associations with advertising and product groups, but that's okay, too.) Evolution is thought of as a slow process (perhaps erroneously, but even that's okay). It happens across an entire species—a collective, an organization—through variations that happen in individuals that prove successful or not.

The organization needs to foster an environment where experiments and variations are welcome, and where the results of those experiments can be understood in context.

Meaningful alignment *must* include adaptation. There has to be a way to adapt, to incorporate new information and iterate upon what is learned.

Adaptation is a reactive process, but it's an iterative one, too. It can be done in stages and cycles. Adaptation doesn't have to be painful.

Be willing to adapt to customer segments as you become aware of them. Even if you don't break out tailored messaging and experiences for those segments right away, identifying them in analytics and reporting on their metrics separately can help begin the transition to treating this group of customers as a meaningfully distinct group with specific motivations and needs.

Make sure feedback truly loops back. If you're getting feedback from customers in support calls, make sure those comments get all the way back to strategists and designers who sit at the beginning of the product and service design process.

Adapt the organization to the new knowledge gradually. Increase the amount of empathy they have for the user because they now have more data about the user.

Build in language that incorporates the new understanding. Debates about political correctness aside, the language we and the people around us use can impact the decisions we make and skew our efforts one way or the other. Hotel brands that decide to refer to customers as "guests" are likely to make subtly different operational decisions than brands that refer to their customers as, well, "customers." In the same way, when experience design leads to insights about the people we interact with, it may be worth noting where our current language misleads us. Here again, as always, seek alignment.

CHAPTER TWELVE

Patterns of Use / Putting It Into Practice

It's all good and well to talk about the metaphors, but how do we put this into practice? I hear you.

The best way to think about these patterns is across industries: For example, in retail, the emerging patterns point to beacons, daily social media presence, and agility. But any business or organization that wants to borrow from what's working in retail can begin to think about ways to implement some of these patterns in their own environment.

In this section we'll look at the patterns and examples common to some of the implementations of integrated physical and digital experience, and how they align with my methodology of Integrated Human Experience Design.

Ownership Versus Access and Privately-Owned Public Spaces

In New York City and other cities like Seattle, Boston, Toronto, and Seoul, commercial real estate developers often make use of a clause that allows them to build beyond their zoning restrictions if they work in public space. It's a phenomenon known as POPS: Privately-Owned Public Space. It's an odd thing to wrap your head around, right? A chunk of public space that is privately owned.

But the digital world has its own version of this weirdness: After all, many of the "places" where we spend time online are privately-owned. Facebook, Twitter, all the social media.

143

We benefit from and make good use of these spaces, but ultimately we are not in control of them. We can access them, but someone else owns them. This is why when they change—such as when Facebook, Twitter, or Instagram pushes out changes to the user interface or to the algorithm that sorts the content feed—it causes great consternation. When both Twitter and Instagram announced disruptions to their chronological feeds in early 2016, people *freaked out.*

Fundamentally, remembering that this disconnect between ownership and access exists has the chance to teach us compassion for those moments. It's easy to scoff at people who get caught up in resisting change. But on some level, they're reacting to that fractured experience.

As physical spaces become more tightly embedded in digital experiences that overlay them, such as with augmented reality, and as digital spaces become aware of and enmeshed in physical places, such as with location-tagging on social media, the disconnects inherent in access-versus-ownership are bound to be more apparent.

For example, after the launch of *Pokémon GO*, Boon and Caro Sheridan found that a stream of people were lingering and converging in front of their home. Of course, their home happened to be an old church they'd renovated. Since many churches were designated as "gyms" for training the characters within the game, players were merely accessing the construct within the game, regardless of ownership. Eventually, Boon and Caro were able to get Niantic, the makers of *Pokémon GO*, to change their home's designation. But the example is a useful precedent for how layered reality may alter our experiences in unexpected ways. (Full disclosure: I know Boon because we both spoke at a user experience conference.)

The access-versus-ownership dilemma is far from new: It's been one of the central issues in the disruption of the entertainment and media industries, due to consumers' shifting priority from owning copies of movies and music to preferring broad on-demand access to a massive catalog of entertainment options. The premise of access over ownership also sits at the foundation of the sharing economy.

The economic and legal impacts of this dilemma are outside the scope of this book, but as experience designers and creators, we have some questions to ask ourselves. For example: How do technological capabilities shift our perspective of the priorities of access over ownership? How does that shift in priorities affect our relationship to place and space? And what obligation do we have, as designers of and sometimes owners of the spaces the public occupies, to remember that change is jarring and to consider the public when introducing changes?

Opportunities for New Cues and Sensory Experiences

It's 10:30 a.m. on an average Wednesday. You're at work, and you start to feel yourself dragging, so you decide to step out for a cup of coffee. You walk down to a local coffee shop, where there's a line to order. You notice a sign at the register showing the store's Instagram handle, so you flick through their Instagram as you stand in line. Their feed is mostly re-shares of customer pictures, which makes you think you should take a picture of your coffee drink when you get yours, too. And now that you think about it, you were planning to order a plain coffee but maybe you should get a cappuccino because the foam is probably more photogenic.

Does it seem ridiculous that such a shallow thing might influence your decision-making? Perhaps for you it is, but subtle cues and nudges have always influenced people's decisions. (See the earlier section on "Cues, Triggers, and Metaphors: Sensory Experience Design" for examples.) The allure of a tiny piece of social fame is a form of validation that is no less compelling than many of the cues marketers have used for ages.

In thinking about the process of leading someone to buy through integrated experiences, we can also consider some emerging cues and sensory experiences, such as:

- proximity
- temperature
- sensory data—smells, auditory cues, etc.

As technologies emerge and digital sophistication increases, we will have expanding opportunities to use metaphors that are still novel for digital. Consider proximity, where a user's experience changes in response to their surroundings and nearby resources; or even sensory cues, such as temperature and other bodily metrics that may indicate meaningful response.

I don't mean to advocate skeuomorphism, although it serves a purpose. Apple has been criticized by designers in some of its operating system versions as leaning too heavily on the visual iconography and interaction metaphors of the physical world to familiarize and dimensionalize their digital counterparts. (For example, using page flips in iBooks; showing thumbnails of books on a virtual wooden bookshelf; making the iOS calculator look like a 1970s model; showing CD iconography in iTunes, etc.) But skeuomorphic designs serve as a transition for new users, giving them cues and handholds into the interactions of a new experience layer.

I certainly don't mean to sound like I'm advocating for manipulation through these sensory cues. There are plenty of examples where that's happening, but that's not an ethical approach to this framework. Still, when we're designing experiences for a business reason, there is a need to be compelling—which requires us to understand what compels.

You could also look to the RFID tags more and more often being affixed to clothes in stores, and the opportunity to use proximity as a cue for an experience. Even temperature is biometric feedback that could potentially be used through wristbands or smart fabrics or other wearables. That could be the trigger for a mood-related or behavior-related experience.

There are other sensory cues—smells, auditory cues, and so on. The data model might not yet support all of the possibilities we can imagine, but we can already be thinking about how to create an expansive experience of the brand and the product.

Just-in-Time Convergence of Physical and Digital

When you think about how the digital and physical worlds are merging, many examples that come to mind have to do with wrapping a digital layer around something that exists in the physical world, whether beacons, connected devices, or even augmented reality. You might not immediately think about how something can start in the digital world and emerge in the physical world. But the additive capabilities of 3-D printing and manufacturing do just that.

There's been steady growth in this area that provides what we might call a just-in-time convergence of the physical and digital. Perhaps more to the point, it's a just-in-time *emergence* of physical matter through digital means.

Emailing a Wrench to Space

On December 22, 2014, something seemingly mundane happened: Someone needed a wrench to fix something. But that someone was NASA Expedition 42 Commander Barry "Butch" Wilmore; and what he needed to fix, in theory, was the International Space Station. So NASA emailed him the specifications, and he printed the ratchet wrench with the on-board 3-D printer.[54]

In other words: humans *emailed* a *wrench* to *space*.

It wasn't for live maintenance; it was just a test of how future missions might handle maintenance needs. But it was a milestone nonetheless.

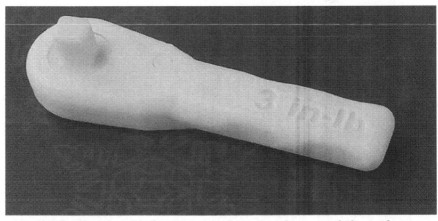

The first hand tool to be 3D printed in space from emailed specifications
(Image source: NASA)

This is one of the most fun examples of the convergence of digital data and the physical world. And best of all, it takes place in SPACE!

3-D/Additive Printing

Aside from maintaining space stations, there are plenty of down-to-earth examples of 3-D printing making exciting things possible.

Printable Fashion

Several designers and cutting-edge startups are using 3-D printing and additive manufacturing to custom-make shoes, or to allow consumers to print their own customized, custom-fit apparel and accessories.

Healthcare

The implications for 3-D printing in healthcare are enormous, offering truly personalized surgical and other medical solutions to patient problems. But the capabilities were perhaps most adorably demonstrated through a veterinary example: by printing a new foot for a duck.

In a classroom duck hatching project, a duck named Buttercup was born with a defective foot. A waterfowl sanctuary took Buttercup in, and they worked with 3-D printing company NovaCopy to print a new foot for Buttercup.

Photo credit: Feathered Angels Waterfowl Sanctuary
via ButtercupTheDuck Facebook page

Of course, human medical treatments are happening, too, from models to implants to custom-made surgical tools. The cost has been one of the barriers to more widespread experimentation and adoption, but is rapidly decreasing to the point where it will begin to make sense in broader applications.

Takeaways for Business

The advent of additive (3-D) printing and manufacturing technology leaves a great deal of room for expansible ideas. Customizations are or will be possible on a scale that wasn't possible before.

Smart Homes and Ambient Tech

More and more data is being collected by "smart" or "connected" devices about our physical beings and surroundings, and this data can be used to affect our surroundings. And if anything blurs the lines between what "online" and "offline" means anymore, it's this kind of tech.

Case in point: Is the Nest thermostat an online or offline device? It's one of many "smart" thermostats. As a physical device, just like any thermostat, it regulates the temperature of a physical space. So it's an offline device, right?

But wait. It's internet-connected, so you can adjust it from your phone or another online connection, so it's an online device.

It's both. Okay, that part was easy.

But here's the blurrier part: The same algorithms that detect patterns in your home's environment and your preferences are also in use in other homes, and over time, the intelligence from all those homes running the same algorithms can be used to fine-tune its performance.

Which means, in other words, it's indirectly connecting your physical environment, virtually, through data, to other people's physical environments.

That's how blurry things are getting, and that blending and crossing over is only the beginning.

***

Home was our starting point for this discussion, and it's appropriate that we return to it here, mid-way, and recognize its own changing role in this landscape. The adoption of integrated digital experiences into the home is well underway. For evidence of this, check out the e-commerce websites of some of the major home improvement retailers. When you think of Home Depot, for example, you probably think of lumber and paint; but as the times change, their inventory has been changing, too. The "smart home" category on their website is loaded with products and subcategories.

The star of the "smart home" category of products and devices is the smart thermostat—it seems to be the one connected home appliance most people can grasp the benefit of right away. But there are also connected locks, like Lockitron and August Smart Lock, which have been available for home use since the early 2010s. These allow the user to lock and unlock their doors from anywhere by using an app, and the locks, detecting the user's proximity through the app using sensors, can unlock the door automatically as the user approaches the house.

Even Amazon Dash belongs in this category. These are single-function re-ordering widgets that mount near a usage context in your home, such as near wherever you keep your paper towels, and allow you to re-order a previously-specified supply of, say, a two-pack of Bounty paper towels. The idea is to let you place an order for a staple product at the moment you realize you're getting low—before you can leave that context, forget about it, and run out completely. Of course, the benefit to Amazon is transparent, but if the Dash buttons help a customer even once to avoid running out of a convenience product, the customer probably appreciates the utility, no matter how heavy-handed the consumerism may be.

You can expect the range of options and uses for smart home devices to continue expanding. And it blurs over into ambient devices as a whole. They're all part of a larger digital mesh, as it's sometimes called. Ambient devices are a category of smart devices that can monitor baseline settings in the physical surroundings and use an internet connection to modify them. That includes sensors around us detecting our presence, as well as the accelerometer in the iPhone that gauges direction, rate, and other dimensions of motion.

The integration of these devices into our surroundings is diverse, ranging from touchable interactive surfaces to biometric recognition, with many of the devices connected and controlled from multiple angles by multiple devices and interfaces.

What's more, this area integrates with 3-D printing and other just-in-time physical emergence from digital cues, because digital cues can be passively received and trigger a physical response. And all of this interacts with the devices and data around you, from autonomous cars and other devices, to algorithms and artificial intelligence.

The duality of this is amazing: Our physical presence is increasingly affected by the technology around us, even as our digital presence is increasingly immersive. There is likely to be no modality of everyday life that will not be affected by a data layer of tracking or modulation.

Your movement follows patterns throughout the day and week, and ambient systems tracking those movements are adapting to those patterns—sometimes through human intervention, such as when analysts review store data about foot paths and optimize the layout—but increasingly those adaptations are algorithmic and part of a machine-learning cycle.

Takeaways for Business

The implication for many businesses isn't just to build smart or connected devices that can track data about physical surroundings and manipulate those surroundings. It's more about being mindful of the nuanced ways that these devices and other platforms and products are blurring the lines between online and offline experiences. Users of these products are becoming increasingly expectant that they will have the opportunity to do things like controlling their home appliances from their phone, or getting usage reports about how their energy consumption compared to the average customer, or seeing their data from one device in context of another device, and so on.

The Human-Centric Data Model: A Look at Airbnb's "Don't Go There; Live There" Campaign

One validation of the idea that deixis and the language of relative place and movement resonates with people (see the section on "The Language of Relative Place and Movement" for more on this) is its use in advertising and marketing communications. Take, for example, the "Don't Go There; Live There" campaign Airbnb introduced in April 2016[55]. The ads argue that "going" somewhere like Paris inherently implies following a visitor's mindset; and limiting your experience of the city to only the most popular attractions—which in many cases are exactly where the *locals* don't go—means missing out on the essence of a place.

Instead, the ads contend, we might set out to get to know the character of a city through its people, its culture, and—this being a promotion for Airbnb, of course—its homes. We might set out to live there, even if, as the voice-over intones, it's only for one night.

It's a very good subtle realization on the part of the company. It twists the language we use to describe the experience of a place to make us more aware of our behavior and our choices.

And for marketers and placemakers in general, it's a good lesson to recognize the layers of context that make up experience.

It's also an interesting take on the meaning of place, and technology's role in facilitating it.

It's the Data Model

In the presentation Airbnb's CEO Brian Chesky gave when he was introducing this "live there" idea at their "Open" event, he showed a side-by-side comparison of the top five recommendations of where to visit as they appear in TripAdvisor (mostly coming from tourists), versus the top five recommendations from Airbnb hosts (who live locally). With the exception of the Jardin du Luxembourg (Luxembourg Gardens—and as a side note, my personal favorite place in Paris), the two lists are different in both content and overall character. Tourists most often recommend the Eiffel Tower, of course, and world-famous museums: the icons of the city. Locals, who perhaps take the icons in stride and prefer to focus on the underlying culture of the city and its inhabitants, recommend a market, a park, a garden, and so on.

The only difference here, in a sense, is the data model. The same places exist in Paris regardless of whether you're collecting the list through TripAdvisor or through Airbnb, but the difference isn't fundamentally about the website that did the collecting or the people who submitted the recommendations: It's what data you use to create the set and rank them. Neither of these lists of recommendations is wrong, but it's about purpose and priority—and meaningfulness. If you want your list to emphasize the tourist perspective (or the "go there" mentality), you might sort for or give weight to the overall popularity of a recommendation; but if you want to emphasize the local's perspective (or the "live there" mentality), you might sort for or give weight to expertise relative to the area.

The key here is that building a service that will be of real value in enhancing a person's experience of place isn't only about marketing the service well; it's about deeply understanding the layers of that experience and how that understanding will be populated out through every facet of the service.

Digital Interactions with Place: The Starbucks App

There are many noble and necessary implementations of the convergence of physical and digital experiences that have to do with public safety, emergency response, access to important resources, and so on. In that perspective, the ability to order a Starbucks soy latte from an iPhone while walking down a Midtown Manhattan street certainly doesn't earn any kind of foundational standing in Maslow's hierarchy of needs, but it's still pretty cool. It's the little details in the Starbucks mobile app that make it such a delightful experience (and one that could easily be studied for fulfilling more humanitarian causes than coffee).

How is the data model supporting human experience here?

It provides unprecedented access to choice, control and visibility of location and timing, plus full integrated payment. All supporting the experience of walking in, skipping the line, and picking up your drink.

* * *

153

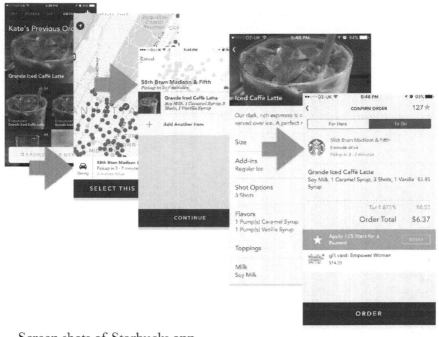

Screen shots of Starbucks app

Customizing orders through kiosks or displays or even apps is not new, but the whole experience design here was particularly well done.

Sure, some of these are not complicated things to get right, but getting a lot of them right together is more rare. Some of them are just nicely executed, such as the juxtaposition of your walk or drive time and your drink prep time. That's the kind of visibility and forethought that we want to provide in converged experiences. Additionally, the fully integrated payment system may not be anything truly groundbreaking, but it's part of the seamlessness of the experience. You're fully specifying your order, you get to see how long it may take you to get to the store to pick it up, you know how long it should take the drink to be prepared, and you're closing out by paying for it, all in one easy process.

The real thing that's happening here that's worth the consideration is that you're walking into the store, bypassing any line at the registers, picking up your drink, and walking out of the store.

That's the real goal: alignment between what Starbucks wants and what customer wants.

That is the goal, not the fact that I can throw three shots of espresso into my drink and customize it with vanilla syrup and caramel syrup and soy milk, though that's all quite nice (if a little excessive, from a caffeine and sugar consumption standpoint). Starbucks benefitted and continues to benefit in a profit sense from its simplifying my ability to customize and order my drink.

The fact that we're both benefiting, that I get to walk in and easily pick up my drink, means I'm now coming back to Starbucks far more often than I otherwise would. It's a more rich and fulfilling experience in my life in this very small way.

So now when I do that, Starbucks is benefiting again and again and again from having been clever in their design of that app.

CHAPTER THIRTEEN

Meaningful Strategies for Integrated Experiences Across Industries

Most of this book so far has examined the human experience at the crossroads of digital data's integration with the physical world. But our examination wouldn't be complete without looking at how that integration will play out across industries—the industries we work in or the businesses we own. These changes aren't only evolving the consumer experience; they're also shaking up what's possible in many areas of business: marketing, manufacturing, operations, and more.

In manufacturing and other heavy industry, the integration of 3-D and additive printing has dramatically changed operations, not to mention the use of robotics and automation.

> "There are three big things in play," said Vish Soaji, GE Digital's head of engineering for industrial IOT application. "Machine learning . . . sensors collecting data, then you combine that data with other types of data to make changes. Second is big data and third is analytics." . . . Meanwhile, Greg Kinsey, vice president of Hitachi Insight Group said Hitachi had identified three areas where IIoT can produce a major impact on the manufacturing sector: smart maintenance; improving quality in production; and dynamic scheduling.[56]

How will automation affect meaning? Between advances in artificial intelligence, robotics, on-demand 3-D manufacturing, and so on, there are huge shifts happening and yet to come in industry, labor, economics, and society. The answer is still not clear.

None of these, of course, have so much to do with connected experiences as they do with implications of connected devices. The experiences come after the fact, after the manufacture, down the supply chain, when the consumers come in contact with the manufactured good. Still, it's helpful to remember that everything we interact with has a data trail, even if we can't experience it; and there will be implications from even the upstream changes and efficiencies of the convergence of physical and digital.

But humans are and will be still in the center of it all, developing the tech, specifying the product, consuming the goods, and ultimately trying to find fulfillment in a model that may obviate one source of their fulfillment: work.

But of course, the more consumer-facing the industry, the more the changes connected experiences bring will be felt.

Beacons, Micro-Location, and Proximity-Based Targeting

The promise of beacons is the ability to engage meaningfully with customers, hotel guests, museum visitors, and people in a variety of other contexts based on: 1) the context of where they are and 2) what marketers and experience designers can infer they might be looking at and interested in because of that. Along with personalized information about, say, a customer's preferences that the retailer might have access to because of purchase history, the aggregate ability to influence purchase behavior through suggestions and tailored displays is tremendous.

There are quite a few companies now manufacturing beacons, including Estimote, Swirl, and GPShopper . . . and of course a little company known as Apple. Though Apple hasn't yet manufactured a physical beacon, they built iBeacon technology into their smartphone and watch devices and integrated it into the iOS7 mobile operating system. As a result, there are an estimated 200 million iOS devices that can serve as transmitters and receivers.[57]

In retail, beacons help retailers respond to behavioral cues from in-store shoppers, in a way parallel to how cookies and tracking data help e-commerce retailers respond to behavioral cues online. Optimizing the store experience around these cues can certainly increase the likelihood that people will buy, while it can also improve people's enjoyment of a store.

Beyond retail, location data and beacons can transform social experiences. For example, Facebook launched a program called Place Tips. According to Facebook, "Your location is determined using cellular networks, Wi-Fi, GPS and Facebook Bluetooth® beacons. Viewing place tips doesn't post on Facebook or show people where you are."

Via Facebook's press release:

> In certain places, we're also testing place tips using Facebook Bluetooth® beacons, which send a signal to your phone that helps us show you the right tips for the right place. We'll be testing these in a handful of businesses in New York such as The Metropolitan Museum of Art, Dominique Ansel Bakery, Strand Book Store, the burger joint at Le Parker Meridien Hotel, Brooklyn Bowl, Pianos, the Big Gay Ice Cream Shop and Veselka.

Businesses can partner with Facebook, exposing statuses posted at the location to people who are currently there. They can also help with navigation in larger stores, in some cases even offering turn-by-turn directions to a desired product, aisle, or section of the store.

They can offer contextually relevant offers and information, based on data and cues that indicate where a customer is in their purchase journey and what previous purchases a customer may have made.

They can help optimize merchandising, allowing for product to be displayed in areas that will see the most foot traffic and where in-store analytics indicate the highest likelihood of sale.

Based on what a customer may have tried on, or how long they lingered in front of something in a store, or what aisle they frequently visit but never buy from, online marketing can continue to serve targeted messages and offers to try to close the deal.

Does some of this get a little creepy? Yes. Most people seem to think so, when asked. A 2015 survey revealed that more than 75 percent of respondents said they would not shop at a store that used facial recognition technology for marketing purposes. However, discounts might be the key to turning consumer perception around, as the number dropped to 55 percent of respondents when they knew there would be a benefit associated with it.[58]

But a bigger issue is that most people don't even fully realize yet what's already happening. In that same 2015 survey, 70 percent of consumers didn't know what in-store beacons were.[59] We don't fully know how people are going to respond as they become aware of beacons and related technology and the privacy considerations that go along with all of them.

However, when the technology is implemented with a healthy dose of respect for the customer's sensibilities and relevant messages are offered, it can go beyond the perception of being a greedy ploy to manipulate customers into spending more money. It can indeed be a huge boon to customers, too, in helping them find the product they're really looking for or that solves a particular problem they might be having.

Large retailers and brands like Macy's, McDonald's, Target, Starbucks, Lord & Taylor, American Eagle Outfitters, Old Navy, Giant Eagle, Universal Music, Apple Stores, and Rite Aid have all implemented beacon technology in various ways. I'll explore a few case studies in the rest of this chapter.

The Check-In, Registration, Onboarding Pattern

Checking in at a desk or some sort of gate authority is a process that happens in healthcare, hospitality, food service, travel, and more. Even retail, museums, universities, and cities have services and functions that relate to this idea.

Take a hotel, for example. When a guest enters the lobby of the hotel, their location can be detected and they might receive a push notification on the hotel's app showing reservation information. All they have to do is confirm the information shown—perhaps simply by swiping the screen—and they are checked in. No waiting in line necessary, no searching for the reservation number.[60] For now, that typically has to happen through a proprietary app or through a platform app like Passbook. But if the guest has the option, this is an especially nice perk in the context of a hotel, since anyone who's been through an airport lately knows there's a pretty good chance the guest has had a long and stressful day of travel.

Although I'm not one to advocate the reduction of human jobs through technological means, it is possible that companies could reallocate some of the staff resources for this function while guests and patients can reduce their wait time. This kind of redistribution of effort opens up the question: what value can human-to-human interaction have that interacting with a screen doesn't offer? What nuance can a person add if they're there to answer questions in person?

Onboarding

When you think about what we can learn from what user experience designers have learned about "onboarding" in digital products and apps, it's interesting to bring that full circle to the term as it relates to getting "on board" a train or a plane. (Yet another metaphor of the physical world in the digital world.)

A good onboarding process in an app or online product not only authenticates the user into the system, but also it orients them to the flow they'll need to take to be successful.

Museums and Interpretation: Holding Space for an Idea

Museums and monuments exist to hold space for an idea. And it stands to reason that in order to convey that idea most effectively, they want to make experiences as immersive as possible for the visitor. How can connected experiences help museums live up to the ideal?

Interpretation and "Tilden's Principles"

In addition to museums, there are integrated experience applications for educational, natural, and recreational resources. With these resources, especially around natural landmarks, comes the field of heritage interpretation. This discipline sometimes incorporates explanatory text, maps, or photographs.

One of the influential voices in the interpretation of natural resources was Freeman Tilden. Tilden established, as one of his six principles of interpretation[61], that "The chief aim of Interpretation is not instruction, but provocation."

Among his other famous quotes:

> "Heritage interpretation is an educational activity which aims to reveal meanings and relationships through the use of original objects, by firsthand experience,and by illustrative media, rather than simply to communicate factual information."

These thoughts lead directly into an appreciation of the meaning of place as key to its appropriate protection, which is perhaps an important idea for cities wrestling with balancing historic preservation with innovation and progress.

In his 1957 book, *Interpreting Our Heritage*, Freeman Tilden defined six principles of interpretation. Here are those principles, interspersed with my own comments:

> 1. Any interpretation that does not somehow relate what is being displayed or described to something within the personality or experience of the visitor will be sterile.

Note: relevance.

> 2. Information, as such, is not Interpretation. Interpretation is revelation based upon information. But they are entirely different things. However all interpretation includes information.

Note: relevance.

> 3. Interpretation is an art, which combines many arts, whether the materials presented are scientific, historical or architectural. Any art is in some degree teachable.

Integration.

> 4. The chief aim of Interpretation is not instruction, but provocation.

Call to action.

> 5. Interpretation should aim to present a whole rather than a part, and must address itself to the whole man rather than any phase.

Holistic.

* * *

> 6. Interpretation addressed to children (say up to the age of twelve) should not be a dilution of the presentation to adults, but should follow a fundamentally different approach. To be at its best it will require a separate program.

Again, relevance. And thus we come to the idea of *meaning* in interpretation.

It is perhaps easy to see how technology that has an awareness of the context of a visitor's movement through place could serve unprecedented functions of mediation and interpretation. Technology could help hold space for the idea as a visitor progresses through an experience by filling out the sensory dimensions of the experience, by enriching the narrative, and by contextualizing time or space or other relationships between elements.

This ties back to the curation discussion because curation, in a sense, is a way of tying threads together between distinct pieces of art or work or culture. Curation and heritage interpretation are different ways of thinking about what is basically the same process. In either case, there are aspects of the content being explored that can always be enriched through technology.

In a physical exhibit, the experience is bound to be linear in at least one way, since a human has to progress from point to point to consume it. So one area for adding richness through technology is through defining a robust metadata model and ensuring that it is complete enough to enhance the content. Providing dimensional attributes about the elements in a collection or exhibit can make for alternate ways of exploring the content and experiencing it.

Technology is poised to make the museum experience even more relevant than it has ever been through personalization, proximity-based experiences, and more.

Beacons can deliver content and experiences based on proximity, which has incredible applications for museums. The experiences can also include interactivity, such as commenting and sharing an exhibit, or games that encourage engagement with the idea of the exhibit or with other visitors, whether they are currently at the museum or have been there previously.

They can monitor "dwell" times—the amount of time visitors spend in front of exhibits—and recommend similar artifacts and products in the museum shop. Curators can use this information to optimize layout.

Certainly the ability to track visitor movement allows for great insights about what exhibits are well-received and which are not getting the exposure or foot traffic.

At the Philips Museum in Eindhoven, The Netherlands, visitors are encouraged to play a game with up to three other players called "Mission Eureka" on an iPad. The game offers the players challenges to solve as they explore, and it reinforces the learning behind the ideas presented in the museum exhibits.

The first museum to use beacons, the National Slate Museum, has at least twenty-five beacons set up throughout the museum that help visitors explore the exhibits and view explanations, just-in-time demonstrations, and more.

In 2014, in observance of the United Nations International Day for Mine Awareness and Assistance in Mine Action, the New Museum in New York City hosted an exhibit that used beacons to simulate a minefield. Created by digital agency Critical Mass along with the United Nations Mine Action Service, the experience asked visitors to download an app called "Sweeper" and wear headphones. The app sensed the visitor's proximity to any of the beacons throughout the exhibit, and triggered a loud audible "detonation" in the visitor's headphones when they approached a virtual land mine. The audio was followed by a recorded testimony of a person's actual experience with land mines. The overall aim was to raise awareness, and visitors were invited to donate five dollars to help ensure that no one else would ever have to go through in real life what they just experienced in digital space.

Healthcare: Healing and Care as Experience

Healthcare is fundamentally about *healing* and *care*. These words are the basis of a lot of the stock language of healthcare, but most of us have experienced situations where the practices don't bear out that ideal in practice.

How can connected experiences help healthcare facilities and services live up to the ideal?

***

* * *

For many people as they age, there's a fierce desire to continue to live as independently as possible, even as certain risks increase—such as falls and the medical complications that can result from them. In fact, the CDC (Centers for Disease Control and Prevention) reports unintentional injury as the leading cause of death in people sixty-five and older, and falls as the leading cause of injury[62]. Of course these risks and outcomes affect the aging person's loved ones, too, so if you have a parent or grandparent who lives independently, it could be a great comfort to you to know that they're safe.

This is why so many companies, from huge enterprises to startups, are developing products and services to monitor senior wellness with connected devices and data services that can alert a caregiver if medication isn't taken, if the senior isn't moving for a while, or even if a routine appliance, like a coffee maker, isn't in use by a certain usual time[63].

Integrated innovations in healthcare aren't all about the elderly, either. People of all ages have embraced the "quantified self" trend since ubiquitous smartphones track their calories, physical activity, sleep quality, and more. Thanks to wearable wristbands and the like, people can monitor an even wider array of biometric and environmental information.

And that's not even taking into account the clinical settings, where there is an enormous variety of connected devices, "smart" equipment, location technology, and access to increasingly rich patient data. Given all this, healthcare is poised to be an industry that can make excellent use of the convergence of physical and digital experiences.

Restaurants and Food Service: Sustenance and Nourishment as

Experiences

At its core, restaurants and food service are about sustenance and nourishment. This is low Maslow's hierarchy stuff, so it's fundamental; but meaning is high Maslow's, so there can sometimes feel like a disconnect between these ideals.

How can connected experiences help restaurants and food service businesses live up to the ideal?

***

The food industry is experiencing a great deal of change due to technology and data. Some pundits refer to the phenomenon of the "Internet of Food," referring to the various ways the supply chain is being augmented with technology and data. There's also the "Internet of the Sea," which refers to commercial fishing, and many other subspecialties of food and technology.

But from an integrated experience perspective, the biggest area of focus is dining.

Sometime in 2015, consumer spending at restaurants overtook grocery stores, and has continued to follow that trend ever since[64].

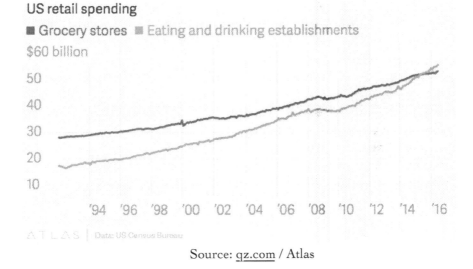

Source: qz.com / Atlas

This means several things. Restaurants and food service businesses may not be the first industry you'd think of for using apps, beacons, and the Internet of Things, but depending on the model, there are quite a few opportunities to address customer frustrations and improve operations. Online reservations are already widespread thanks to platforms like OpenTable, and now the food service industry is addressing some of the other pain points.

If you measure the consumption of food not by money but by calories, what Americans consume away from home has increased from 18 percent away from home in 1978 to 32 percent in 2008. In general, food consumed away from home is higher in salt, saturated fat, and sodium, while it is lower in dietary fiber. It's no surprise, then, that some studies cite the increase in American dining out as a potential contributor to the rise in US obesity.

There's also a tremendous opportunity to increase awareness of healthy options on menus through interactive ordering and allowing customers to customize their orders from the app. If the customer can visualize how skipping a side of sour cream might save them 100 calories and 12 grams of fat, they might just pass. And that could ultimately cut down on food waste at restaurants, too.

Pre-Visit Ordering or Order from Table

One area where customer frustration and restaurant inefficiency overlap is in the time it takes a server to take the table's order. Depending on the model, this step might be about placing the order and paying for it online to be served table-side, or it might include ordering food at the table once the customer arrives at the restaurant or, in some cases, if a beacon detects the customer's reservation. Once the customer is seated, the beacon can trigger the app to display a menu, allowing the customer to review the details of the dishes, including nutrition, price, and customer reviews. Restaurants can offer this service inside of their own apps, or use third-party apps like Allset to address the time people spend waiting around at restaurants, using online ordering to expedite the process of getting food to patrons once they've been seated.

So far the third-party apps are charging a flat fee or a percentage on the order that is passed on to customers, although other models could potentially work. In the meantime, pre-visit ordering addresses a customer frustration while also accelerating table turnover within restaurants, which could mean potentially greater profits.

Check-In

Given the same model of using a beacon to trigger a push notification in an app, a restaurant could push a welcome message to a customer showing their loyalty points.

In some cases, the customer can then even choose where to sit. Forget tipping the maître d' for the best seats in the house.

Promotions, Rewards, and Loyalty

Of course, these technologies will certainly be used to promote specials and will offer discounts to entice customers to visit more frequently or spend more money. They can also integrate with social media and reward customers for social shares of food pictures, location check-ins, and campaign promotions. These social rewards can even be used for discounts or specials, whether through the restaurant's own branded platform or through a third-party like Yelp, Foursquare, or others. With customers whose order histories and preferences are known, the restaurant can offer tailored promotions around their favorite dishes, as well as the option to use reward points toward certain dishes.

Wait Time

Interactive ordering has one more potential advantage: letting hungry diners know when they can expect their food to be served. Systems that integrate back-of-house operations into relevant displays on the user interface could reduce customer anxiety and increase overall satisfaction in the dining experience.

In addition, the app could help the customer multitasking during their wait by providing additional content. Depending on the style and brand characteristics of the restaurant, that could take the form of, say, trivia about the restaurant's city, sports news and scores in a sports bar, or perhaps in a family-oriented establishment, quizzes and games families could play together while they wait.

Payment

The final piece of the puzzle is key: payment. The restaurant could digitally send the bill for the food to the patron's phone or device, from which the customer could settle up and then easily leave the restaurant without having to wait for the server, also freeing the server up to tend to other tables.

Hospitality: Making Guests Feel at Home, Only Better

Hotels and other hospitality businesses are fundamentally about creating a sense of home away from home. We've already explored some of the notions of home. So how can connected experiences help hotels and other hospitality businesses live up to the ideal?

Of course different hotel brands all have different characteristics. Those which are geared toward the frequent business traveler are often situated near airports, for example; and they focus on making amenities convenient and accessible. Such branded hotels have the opportunity to highlight different kinds of conveniences through their integrated experiences.

Upgrade and Upsell

A lot goes through a person's mind as they cross the threshold of the hotel where they'll be spending the next few nights of their life. Depending on what past experiences have taught you to expect, it's either a moment of mild anxiety or a moment of hope, or more likely a little of both. If an arriving guest is toying with the idea of a bigger room, a better view, a more inclusive package, or any other upgrade they haven't indulged in yet, this is the hotel's last best shot at encouraging them to spring for it.

Finding the Guest Room and Other Indoor Navigation

We all know hotels and resorts aren't actually home, but the business they're in, in a sense, is of making us feel almost as comfortable as being at home, or at least distracting us from what we're missing at home.

The technology a hotel might use for wayfinding and navigation, such as beacons, could serve additional purposes. They could provide context about art and exhibits throughout the building, or provide an interactive tour of the resort with turn-by-turn directions and virtual maps.

The James Hotels uses iBeacon integration in the James Pocket

Assistant app and beacons throughout their properties to offer guests a "self-guided" tour of the hotels' art collections.

Keyless Room Entry and Security

While we're at it, once the guest has checked in without having to go to the front desk, hotels could also potentially do away with hotel room keys and key cards. By allowing a beacon technology to detect the their smartphone, the guest could approach the room and unlock the door automatically.

Keyless entry (when it works) is a great convenience, saving the guest from having to fumble around in their wallet or bag to retrieve a key. It could arguably be safer and more secure. As a woman who often travels alone, I am conscious of the ways in which my room location and access is compromised during the normal course of a hotel stay. A front desk clerk may announce the room number out loud to me with other people nearby, or they may hand me a key card in a paper jacket marked with the room number. This paper jacket is something I could easily misplace, leaving my room vulnerable. If my check-in process takes place on my phone screen, with no audible announcement of my room number, and room access is linked to my phone as well, there seems to be a much better chance that my room remains private and secure. Or at least I'll *feel* that I'm more secure, which is a big step in creating the intended experience anyway.

Starwood Hotels and Resorts implemented a pilot program in January 2014 in two major hotel locations—Manhattan and Silicon Valley—to test out providing guests with keyless entry. The guests first had to install the Starwood Preferred Guest (SGP) app, but then they had access to a virtual key. Through Bluetooth 4.0, they could access their rooms with a tap of their smartphones. They've since then rolled out beacons in dozens of additional hotel locations.

Beyond frictionless check-in and keyless room entry, this infrastructure in hotels can mean a more personalized experience where at a minimum staff can greet guests by name, if that aligns with the brand. It also lends itself to more subtle service customizations, such as, for example, the cleaning staff knowing when guests are in their room and not. It makes "do not disturb" door hangers seem quaint.

In-Room Controls

In an effort to conserve energy, many hotels, especially in Europe, require guests to enter or swipe a key card to turn on the lights. Beacons make that unnecessary: If the guests have logged in through the app on their smartphone or tablet, the beacon can sense their proximity and allow control of lighting and other features of the room, including the TV and the temperature. This can all potentially be controlled right from the app.

Relevant Room Service

Another convenience made possible through the connection between beacons and apps is room service. If the guest is in the room as a meal time approaches, the beacon may be able to detect the phone's presence and push a notification about the special of the day. The push could ask the guest if they would like to order something. What's more, at some point when booking the room or completing their loyalty program signup, the guest may have indicated their dietary preferences; and the app could make tailored suggestions. (As a frequent traveler who has also been vegan for the past twenty years, I can tell you that this is a data-driven convenience I would welcome.) The app might also include compelling interactive features on how the ingredients are sourced, how the food is prepared, and so on.

Targeted Offers for On-Site Retail and Dining

If you've ever stayed in one of the big hotels on or anywhere near the Las Vegas Strip, you've no doubt seen examples of how on-site retail and dining can add color to the overall hotel brand and experience. For example, on the 16.7-acre grounds of the Hard Rock Hotel and Casino, the shops and dining options include an Affliction store, a John Varvatos store, a cantina-inspired eatery called Pink Taco, and a twenty-four-hour diner called Mr. Lucky's. Whether your personal taste delights in or recoils at what the sum of that aggregate brand comes out to be, you can probably acknowledge that these retail and dining components are contributing something to it.

Beacons can alert guests as they near a venue, where they may receive a targeted offer or special discount. These offers can be based on customizations the guest entered in advance, or that adjust with the guest's history and as the guest responds to offers. Drink coupons, discounts at shops, deals on show tickets, and more—they can not only be offered, but also *strategically* offered when the guest is most likely to accept and use the deal. Proximity is as good a starting point for that strategy as anything.

Even in mainstream chain hotels, retail and dining are big parts of the overall guest engagement strategy. Smaller airport hotels that cater to business travelers often feature convenience stores that sell toiletries, snacks, phone chargers, and other easily forgotten small necessities. Some hotels even offer complimentary toothbrushes, razors, and so on. Whether included or extra, the hotel's app can make replacing these items a simple matter of checking them from a list, and having them delivered to the door.

Expedited Check-Out

Just as beacons and smartphones can streamline check-in, they can also streamline check-out. On the morning the guest is due to depart, their phone can prompt them to check out digitally and can even give them the option to extend their stay. Then, once again without having to stand in line at the front desk, they can review and confirm their receipt and have it emailed to their address.

Everything Everywhere

Neither retail nor education nor healthcare nor much of anything takes place exclusively in the physical places—stores, schools, hospitals, etc.—that are reserved for them. So a big movement in many of these industries, and maybe in yours, is to have everything be available from everywhere, yet with context-awareness, location sensitivity, and targeted offers.

For example, the travel experience isn't limited to airplanes and hotels; travelers often want to explore, and the savvy travel brands can use this opportunity to engage meaningfully with them with recommendations and resources, such as a wearable device like a bracelet that could help alert them to any traveler-friendly places (such as restaurants, pubs, gyms, or community centers).

Retailers have had to adopt a "retail is everywhere" mindset, along with the capacity to integrate with wearables for payment, authentication, and even emotional tracking related to purchase behavior.

> "Retail is everywhere, and no longer about a location or a channel."
> — Patricia Walker, senior managing director of products and North America retail practice lead at Accenture

Healthcare is happening everywhere, too: With hospital occupancy rates long in decline—from 77 percent national inpatient occupancy rate in 1980 to only 60 percent in 2013[65]—and with regulation for reimbursement tightening[66], hospital companies have been shifting services to outpatient care for years. Combined with the consumer trend for internet self-diagnosis and the growth of physicians offering services outside of the hospital, these dynamics have set the stage for significant changes to patient care. Any comprehensive look at healthcare must now include telehealth services, where providers offer consultations remotely via computer or phone; patient research online in medical websites and on social media; patient data from wearables; big data analysis[67]; and more.

But quality of care is another question. As anyone who's ever Googled their symptoms knows, every possible diagnosis includes cancer or imminent death. More critically, protecting patient health data is a must, and that doesn't change no matter how the care is offered.

The data safety consideration of this everything-all-the-time imperative can easily become challenging in any application. Such has been the case with the controversy surrounding New York City's LinkNYC program, aimed at replacing 7,500 old pay phones with "new structures called Links. Each Link will provide superfast, free public Wi-Fi, phone calls, device charging and a tablet for Internet browsing, access to city services, maps and directions."[68]

But the initiative has been criticized for how certain aspects of the kiosks could expose users to hackers, its corporate ties and heritage, its carte blanche access to user data, and its ability to use that data to target advertising, which is what pays for the $200 million program.[69]

The legitimacy of any of these criticisms is subject to debate, but the lesson remains: Anytime a project attempts to use personal data to offer goods or services, there are going to be more far-reaching considerations than how quickly it pays for itself. Smart cities and the tools they introduce could potentially do a lot of good, but simply collecting a lot of data from connected devices and then targeting advertising to it is the kind of model that inherently invites scrutiny. We've all de facto agreed to an advertising-driven model of content presentation; now it's just a question of degree. The LinkNYC kiosks may be on the far side of that spectrum of degree, but they're not without precedent.

And to some extent or other, every implementation of integrated experience that attempts to be always-on and tuned to cues in the person's environment is dancing along the cliff edge of what we've agreed to in the implicit social contract about sharing and using our data. But the need for privacy and security is real, just as the overall trend is toward decentralization of services into a more conceptual experience of the "place" in which people experience those services. We must align our organizations' futures with that of the people we serve, which means protecting their data safety while providing quality service that is relevant and contextual, wherever they happen to be.

Retail: Transcending the Transactional and Creating Value Beyond

the Purchase

Retail, at its core, is about experiences that transcend the transactional. Creating a sense of value that goes beyond the purchase.

How can connected experiences help retailers live up to the ideal?

Retail has been the proving ground of the convergence of physical space and digital experience, and the future of retail depends on its continuing to hybridize the experiences. The industry's hand has been forced by the sharp ascent of e-commerce over the past two decades. A June 2015 McKinsey Global Institute report found that IoT is forecasted to have a total economic impact between $3.9 and $11.1 trillion a year by 2025. Of that, $410 billion to $1.2 trillion per year will be implemented in retail environments, between self-checkout technologies, merchandise layout optimization, smart customer-relationship management applications, and more.[70] Not only this, according to recent Juniper Research, retailers are predicted to invest $2.5 billion in IoT by 2020, nearly four times their 2015 investment. Much of that investment will be in iBeacon Technology and RFID.[71]

Showrooming and Webrooming

In the first wave, the so-called "brick and mortar" store experience was almost thought to be a liability. With some understanding of how to converge some of the best of both worlds, "bricks and clicks" was born. But with this phenomenon came an understanding of the concept of "showrooming," where consumers visited a physical store to experience a product (such as shoes or apparel) in person; tried the product on to limit the inconvenience of dealing with the prospect of returning an item through shipping services; then purchased the product online, where prices might be lower, or selection might be broader. According to a 2015 Accenture report, 65 percent of US shoppers are likely to participate in showrooming.[72]

But in time we recognized the growth of "webrooming," too, where consumers used the internet to research products and even purchase them, but chose to complete their purchase or simply pick the product up in a physical store. This is most likely motivated by the convenience and instant gratification of immediate pickup. Perhaps surprising, the percentage of US shoppers likely to participate in webrooming is even higher than showrooming according to the same Accenture report: 69 percent. Think of purchasing a new laptop at the Apple Store, for example. The advantage to this from a consumer's perspective might be the opportunity to ensure the exact desired product is available, and obtain the product the same day. Or the customer can get a custom code sent by email or SMS to pick up their merchandise from a storage locker, sometimes located outside the store so that it can be accessed at the customer's convenience, at any time of day or night.

Click and Collect; In-Store Pickup Services; BOPIS

Customers can place orders online and pick up the product at a time convenient for them, even after the store's closing if the store offers lockers. This is known as buy online, pick up in-store (BOPIS). Beacons can further improve this customer experience by signaling to an associate when a customer who has ordered a product online has entered the store, so the associate can tend to them quickly.

Targeted Offers

With customer data from online and in-store combined, retailers have unprecedented insights about what makes people decide to buy. They can use this to offer increasingly personalized messages.

Target rolled out beacons to fifty stores in 2015, and while other retailers have had to experiment and adapt their practices from trial and perhaps error, Target has been proactive in determining what its approach will be, perhaps informed by observing other retailers' experiments. For example, they specify that they will present no more than two messages per device per shopping trip. "And we'll make sure the alerts and in-app updates provide compelling content and offers," the company said in its news release.

They've already been using app-based in-store commerce for several years, having rolled out Shopkick's rewards app at all 1,700 locations in 2012. This allows consumers to scan products in Target's aisles to redeem discounts known as "kicks" from Target gift cards, Facebook credits, dining gift certificates, iTunes downloads, donations to charities, and other sites.[73]

Smarter Showrooms

By embracing this trend and working with the technology available, retailers can do innovative things. In Toronto in May 2016, IKEA staged a pop-up showroom using augmented reality and Google Cardboard viewers for digital exploration in physical space, which meant that visitors could, according to IKEA's web page about the event, "experience four different IKEA kitchens with virtual reality showcasing various door fronts, cabinets, appliances, sinks, storage solutions and more."[74]

Online Trying Out Offline Presence

Here and there, we're seeing online models that are dipping toes into the waters of offline.

Amazon has been opening brick-and-mortar bookstores.[75] Casper, the mattress company, has been an interesting case study with not only its retail "apartment" showroom[76], where New Yorkers can see and try the mattress in the context of an apartment setting, but also their mobile "Nap Tour" truck[77] that appeared in cities across the United States. Rent the Runway opened four physical stores in 2015, which prompted their traffic to spike: their unique visits increased by 100K in one year.[78]

Social Media Location Sharing

Both pop-up stores and retail trucks must rely on something other than people's knowledge of them to draw customers. They need to communicate their existence by some means to potential customers who might be nearby and interested. For most of the early 2010s, Twitter has been a nearly ideal channel for this, as its timeline was chronological (until early 2016); and the way users tended to consume Twitter content was transitory, so if a retailer posted a location one day but was in a different spot the next, it wasn't too likely that the content would be confusing for prospective customers. Since Twitter introduced an algorithmically-driven timeline, however, that dynamic is changing. Meanwhile, other options have been emerging, including Snapchat, which skews toward a younger demographic who may be more familiar with and predisposed to using pop-up and mobile options anyway.

Operational Efficiencies

Besides the opportunities to engage more relevantly with customers, other uses of IoT, RFID, and beacons in retail have more to do with cost reduction through operational efficiencies. RFID is being deployed in many environments to track sales trends and create a smarter supply chain.

In-Store Analytics Tools; Service Market Growing

One indicator that this physical and digital convergence is happening in retail is that the tools and service market for in-store analytics is growing.

Walkbase, the provider of in-store analytics for airports and retail stores, announced that it has continued its record breaking growth in 2015, analyzing the in-store habits of over one hundred million shoppers to date, compared to fifty million shoppers the year before. The company also saw the value of its customer contract base grow ten-fold with its platform now servicing thirty major retailers in UK and Europe.

Loyalty

Retailers are turning to data to engage with customers about their actual actions and purchases on a granular level and reward them for their loyalty to a specific product or product line. This level of attention to customized loyalty can mean great returns for the retailer, and can yield sweet discounts for a product-loyal customer.

Smart Fitting Rooms

From a convenience perspective, e-commerce generally has obvious advantages over brick-and-mortar shopping, since you can do it from your bed, your desk, your morning jog—wherever and whenever. Of course when it comes to buying clothes, one of the reasons the physical in-store experience has traditionally beat out the e-commerce experience has to do with the ability to try items on and see how they fit, how they look, and what they feel like. On the other hand, if you have to decide between a few sizes or a few colors, or both, the actual process of using a fitting room to try clothes on—disrobing and getting dressed over and over again—can quickly become tedious. Since this area of the store is both a weakness and a strength, it's been a natural focus of many retailers' attempts at innovation.

There are quite a few variations on this idea.

* * *

Images via YouTube

One of the approaches has to do with embedding radio-frequency identification (RFID) in clothing price tags, so that technology in the fitting room can detect which items have been brought in and provide contextual information on an interactive display that also allows the consumer to review styling options or other products entirely. Some systems allow customers to log into their store accounts integrated with e-commerce systems, add items to online wishlists, and sign up for notices when the item goes on sale. They could be integrated with inventory in the store location and across nearby locations. They could show alternate sizing and colors of the items the customer has picked out, so that if the customer would like to try alternate sizing or colors, they could simply select them and alert a store associate to bring the items to the fitting room.[79]

Bloomingdale's installed iPads in its fitting rooms in 2014 to allow the customer to signal an associate if they wanted a different size or color. Some retailers' systems can even allow the purchase of the products right from the fitting room screen.

Another variation on "smart" fitting rooms is smart or "magic" mirrors. Some retailers are installing mirrors that provide a 360-degree view of the outfit, and some provide options for alternate lighting conditions. Fashion design brand Rebecca Minkoff has mirrors that allow customers control of the lighting, in a range of New York City–branded scenarios from "Brooklyn Morning" to "SoHo After Dark." Topshop has a mirror that uses built-in cameras to track the customer's body and project the clothes virtually on-screen, so that the customer doesn't even need to get undressed to try on clothes. [80]

In a few cases, these "magic mirrors" have been equipped with motion sensors and algorithms that can recognize the patterns of customer facial expressions and bodily features. These may detect when customers are feeling uncertain about the item. In such a case, the mirror could actually produce a compliment from a range of possibilities, flattering the customer on their taste in clothes, perhaps even complimenting them on their hair.

This kind of machine-driven mirror offering emotional feedback is an uncanny valley version of the all-reassuring salesperson who tells the customer they look good in what they're trying on no matter what. Is this progress? Who can say. But it's happening, and it's important to know that the technology exists.

Some of this is about empowering the person who's shopping to feel like they have more agency in the process than they've had in the past, and some of it is allowing the in-store experience to rival or even improve on the online shopping experience. All of it has the potential to go too far and make customers uncomfortable, so success in implementing these will depend on designing the experience in alignment with both business outcomes and a sensitivity to the customers' threshold for envelope-pushing experiences.

In retail, we know we need to sell products, but we also know that we run the risk of overstepping the line. "Smart" dressing room mirrors that allow a customer to adjust the lighting in the room are fairly well aligned with realistic customer needs, but mirrors that use facial recognition algorithms to detect micro-expressions of uncertainty and pay compliments to hesitant customers? That seems to cross the line into outright manipulation.

At what cost do we make the sale?

Even just considering profitability, not ethics, you have to think that forcing a sale potentially costs you the long-term loyalty of that customer.

Sometimes conversion rates are high because of persuasive tactics, but conversion rate don't always tell the full story: they don't always take into account return rates, or customer satisfaction rates, or net promoter score, or the elusive, difficult-to-measure concept of buyers remorse. It's worth consideration when and whether our purposes are truly aligned with our customers to ensure ongoing success.

Going Where the Customers Are: Food Trucks, Fashion Trucks

Borrowing from the food truck trend, converted vans, campers, and trucks are now housing small retailers. As with pop-up stores, sometimes larger retail brands spin up.

Similarly, the disruption to the point-of-sale in the form of Square, Apple Pay, and other mobile and digital processors is lowering the barrier to entry for small businesses and is facilitating mobility. It can be no coincidence that the number of businesses operating out of trucks, such as food and fashion trucks, grew dramatically in the years following the introduction of Square Reader and Register in 2010. When you don't need conventional hardware to conduct transactions, you can operate unconventionally. The continued movement in that direction will only disrupt more industries, and for good. In evolutionary terms, a dramatically changing landscape creates the environment for hardy new species, just as successful species change the landscape.

It's rarely just one environmental factor at play, though. Taking an even closer look at food trucks, according to IBISWorld, they represent an $804M industry that has seen 12.4 percent annual growth from 2009 through 2014. Emergent Research projects that will grow to $2.7 billion by 2017. The numbers really started to flourish around the time the economy tanked; as it turns out, food trucks are a great demonstration of the Lean Start-up idea of "minimum viable product." Investors unwilling to bet on a brick-and-mortar restaurant might take a chance on a restaurateur demonstrating proof of concept at lower overhead. So the timing is a reflection of the economy, but that skyrocketing growth has been heavily led by the prevalence of social media and connected consumers who can learn about a truck's location with a tweet. Again, the landscape and the species are related.

A 2013 survey by NPD Group suggests that many consumers (about half of those surveyed) opting for food trucks were replacing a meal in which they might have eaten at a quick service restaurant (QSR)—in other words, at least in 2013, food trucks were the new fast food.[81]

Moreover, in addition to the recession and the proliferation of social media, the popularity of food trucks was also informed by the overlapping trends of "New Localism," which is growing consumer interest in supporting local business; a rise in local food movements, in which consumers demonstrate concern over food origins by preferring locally and regionally grown goods; and The New Artisans movement, which are people starting businesses focused on creating high-quality, hand-produced goods with an emphasis on authenticity.

All of this is driven by an adaptive approach to place coupled with digital discovery.

Payment Disruption and the Virtualization of Value

Value has been virtual for as long as we've had trade. And pre-internet virtual value exchange happened through credit cards. And personal checks. Even cash, when you think about it, is virtual.

But now payment is increasingly integrated with convenience systems. Through the food ordering app Seamless, you place your order, pay for it, *and* tip the delivery person all from your home or office or wherever, all before it ever leaves the restaurant to arrive at your door. Streamlining that process blends together the convenience of the app's interface, the efficiency of the service, and the quality of the food from whatever restaurant you choose. It is all one experience.

One of the big changes in the retail landscape has to do with payment. There are so many payment disruptions in the past few years, from Bitcoin and other cryptocurrency to payment via virtual "gift card" on mobile app, to the way Starbucks and other brands have done it. In all, customers are definitely starting to expect some form of "easy pay," where, rather than paying with cash, check, or credit cards, the customer can use a mobile phone in some way to pay for good or services.

With mainstream retailers like Whole Foods and Target adopting Apple Pay, that platform seems poised to achieve widespread acceptance in the coming years. What that will mean about privacy and behavioral targeting is still unknown.

Having payment go virtual changes a lot about the context in which people think about their money. It makes money more abstract, and people may be willing to spend more.

It's already been shown that people who pay with a credit card tend to focus on the benefit of the purchase, whereas people paying with cash focus on the cost[82]. How will this play out with other virtual forms of payment, like payments integrated into apps? Or in-app purchases using token currency, such as in games? Or Bitcoin?

Rather than seeing this as an opportunity to manipulate customers out of more money, it may be an opportunity to innovate. Again, citing Starbucks: The way customers are presented with their loyalty program in the app, the payment is further removed from a cash concept.

The question, then, is: How do each of the brand stakeholders in that Seamless value chain, for instance, differentiate their value from other options?

The restaurants that have the resources will build their own integrated apps, and many are already doing so. But with dedicated apps, there's a value that has to be proven about having a dedicated app for one restaurant, rather than using an app that aggregates many restaurant options.

It gets complicated.

In any case, we still have to think about value exchange. If money is made more abstract for customers, then quite likely value is too. It's imperative to reinforce the value of the experience they're taking part in. That might mean sending an email congratulating the person on their purchase and offering tips on care of the product, or it might mean reinforcing the values of the brand at the point of purchase. For example, Nespresso wants to counter the idea that pods are environmentally damaging, so one of the parts of the purchase dialogue is for the brand representative to offer the customer a recycling bag for their used pods. Even if the customer declines the bag or never uses it, the brand has reinforced the idea of the value through the experience. Further digital follow-up about recycling might further reinforce this idea, and it might drive loyalty as well.

Pop-Up Retail and Dining Concepts

One of the more liberating trends to emerge for retail in the past decade is that of pop-up stores. The origins of these fleeting retail experiences owe partly to street vendors, craft fairs, and art installations. And many were simply an economical option to sell goods while utilizing available commercial real estate in transitory ways. In cities around the world, though, this now happens every day in a wide range of ways, and technology is becoming an increasingly important part both of spreading the word and creating the experience.

> The street label Airwalk launched the first invisible pop-ups in 2010: Customers downloaded an app and headed to specified public locations where they could access virtual galleries of sneakers using their smartphones.[83]

Pop-up stores have also become a sort of clearing-house for conceptually-related products. Even global brands have latched onto the concept for seasonal and thematic shops. Consider Target, with their sixteen-thousand-square-foot "Target Wonderland" holiday store concept in Manhattan's Meatpacking District in 2015. It was a toy-themed, playground-like experience, but it was also an opportunity for proof of concept for retail experiences that could make it into mainstream Target retail stores full-time. Visitors to the pop-up store were given RFID key fobs instead of carts, and they could swipe these over any items they wanted to purchase. But the tracking on these key fobs allowed Target to analyze patterns of shopper movement throughout the environment, and spot any opportunities for optimizing the merchandising and layout of regular stores.

By combining pop-up stores with beacon technology, retailers can try to orient customers in an unfamiliar store and offer innovative experiences.

Navigation and Wayfinding, Outdoors and Indoors

GPS works great for road navigation, but it's typically not very effective indoors—for example, inside a hotel, museum, shopping mall, hospital, convention center, or casino. Guests need to know where to find a particular store in the mall, a designated meeting room in the convention center, a specific roulette table in the casino. Yet these large spaces require guests to navigate unfamiliar spaces to make best use of the grounds.

It doesn't help that these gigantic and often overwhelming spaces don't always have distinct visual landmarks inside, or any way for a guest to get their bearings and find their way around. So a meaningful use of integrated experience design in these spaces might be to provide contextual guidance on an as-needed basis. Using the hotel as an example, beacons can serve this function by using geo-fenced areas of the grounds to determine where the guest is and offer guidance to their room, the fitness center, the restaurant inside the hotel, and so on.

Digital signage can be a critically important piece of the success of wayfinding in retail, museums, healthcare, cities, event venues, and more.

When a customer approaches, beacons can trigger digital signage to display relevant content based on purchase behavior, other journey insights, and browse patterns through the store.

It can act as an auxiliary screen if the customer has their phone in their pocket or purse, pushing what would be mobile notifications to the digital signage display.

Patterns: Cities, Urban Design, Urban Planning

Cities are rich with metaphors of place, and from them we can derive lessons for integrated experience about community, engagement, identity, culture, and growth. In addition, of course, cities are *places* in their own right, with integrated experience design challenges of their own.

I love cities. I love the sense of energy they collect and distribute from the people who inhabit them. That kind of palpable energy can really only happen in dense environments.

So when I think about what cities *are*, that's one of the key ideas that always surfaces.

It also makes me consider what density feels like online, and what a dense online place has to offer its population. A social network like Tumblr, for example, with a high daily returning visit rate, does seem almost to give off a sense of energy—all the more so if you were to compare it with a deserted chat forum where the last post and comments were from 2004.

But that's only one of many parallels we can draw and examine between cities and online spaces and communities.

In a city, a great deal of effort goes into balancing preservation of history with progress. Different cities lean different ways on the preservation-progress spectrum. Paris, aside from the La Défense business district, is almost entirely preservation, while say Shanghai, with the exception of a few notable historic buildings and areas, seems with its skyscrapers and cranes to be pegged to progress.

Likewise, the contrast in online spaces and tools could scarcely be better illustrated than with Flickr on the side of history, as it is practically synonymous with "archive," not active usage. And on the side of progress, we have Snapchat, with its youthful user demographics and lightweight augmented reality features like lens and geofilters—social media toys, for all intents and purposes. Everything about the platform all but promises something even more fun and innovative to happen in the future.

But what about the people in the mix of all this history and progress?

It's tough to separate community from the place where community forms. So it's important to preserve some sense of the buildings and cityscape that shaped the community. But it's also important to introduce new ideas to keep the community growing and moving forward with advancements in society and culture. A community that gets out of step with the society and culture around it is at risk of being cut off. Intentional placemaking can help restore and preserve the functions of historic buildings and urban districts[84]. That means continuity for the community.

The same may be true online, too.

Data and digital connectedness in communities like Twitter, Facebook, and other gathering spaces link a communities inhabitants across time. And data and digital connectedness link a city's inhabitants across time, too, often through these same channels.

In the next section, we'll examine some patterns and practices for adopting integration of physical and digital experiences from cities around the world.

Cities and The Smart City Imperative

The notion of smart cities is alluring, as it promises conveniences and advancements we've seen imagined in science fiction. A great deal of opportunities are already available with what is possible today, but it takes most cities a herculean effort of bureaucracy to muster the changes to civic infrastructure needed to take advantage of them. Still, a great many initiatives are underway, some sponsored by corporate giants like Google and IBM who have products and services geared at cities (and who stand to benefit from a more connected populace).

We can think of the Internet of Things in this context, not so much as smart refrigerators and smart toasters, but instead as IP-enabled embedded devices connected to the Internet—including sensors, machines, active positioning tags, radio-frequency identification (RFID) readers, building automation equipment, and much more.

Some of the most promising applications of data and the Internet of Things as they are being applied and will be applied in cities have to do with:

- Assistance for residents and visitors who are disabled and differently-abled, such as those with visual impairments, through location data and beacon guidance and other technology enhancements to wayfinding and navigation
- "Smart" parking alerts and monitoring to assist drivers in finding nearby spaces to save their time, maximize parking utilization, and decrease the amount of greenhouse gases being emitted by cars circling blocks looking for a parking spot
- Transit reliability and predictability have huge impacts, too, and will be of particular value to the city's lower-income residents who rely on public transit

I saw the latter play out in Chicago, along Michigan Avenue. Bus shelters everywhere tend to have a list of routes that stop at the station, so that's nothing new; but these shelters included digital displays showing the buses en route to the station and how long before each arrived. That technology is in place in other cities, and in other infrastructure in other cities. For example, most of New York City's subway stations include signs that show which trains are approaching and when, and NYC's MTA does track that data for buses and makes it accessible online but not visibly at the stops and shelters. That said, the buses are what connect people across the grid at a most granular level, and many cities, including NYC, are missing this level of signage for buses to allow riders better ability to plan their routes and arrival time.

This is a basic, fairly low-level implementation of data in place, but whereas many tech advances benefit the wealthy and privileged first, this is an initiative that cuts across socioeconomic classes and helps the lower-income and working classes who often depend more heavily on public transportation.

Elements of Smart Cities

When we talk about smart cities, we're really talking about a combination of any of the following elements or more:

- Traffic flow enhancement, where sensors can not only monitor traffic flow, as they already do, but along with predictive analytics, can trigger alerts to be sent to drivers to seek alternate routes when certain routes are congested.
- Smart services, like parking and transit enhancements. For example, data could inform the driver of—or, in an autonomous vehicle context, simply guide the car to—available parking spaces, the selection of which can be optimized for either proximity to destination or lowest overall price. If the parking app is granted visibility into the driver/passenger's calendar, of course, it potentially makes the decision seamless.
- Smart environment, such as monitoring pollution levels, measuring tremor levels for earthquakes, and sending relevant notifications to citizens about relevant issues.
- Smart security, such as home and building automation that is guided remotely and/or by data-based rules.
- Structural health, where buildings can self-report the need for maintenance issues, along with other necessary information.
- Smart logistics, which encompasses a wide range of intelligent data-driven services for a variety of purposes—like triggering garbage trucks to come around and empty bins when a sensor reports that they are full—to improve the living conditions for citizens and reduce maintenance costs for cities.
- And to some extent, the decentralization and/or democratization of public places.

These may be achieved through a combination of sensors, location-aware services, ubiquitous or widespread open mobile access everywhere, and other technologies.

Public/Private Partnerships

Increasingly, open data projects are being funded through public/private partnerships.

This makes the infrastructure available in a timeline and scale that might not be possible with taxes or civic budgets, and it can be seen as goodwill for the company that sponsors it. Google and their Fiber program are one such example, where putting high-speed internet in place in cities across the country (and around the world) may be only marginally profitable for them; but ensuring that as many people as possible can use data-rich services ultimately means that their data stores are richer. For a company that monetizes data in a wide variety of ways, that could well be worth the investment.

In 2016, Siemens announced a partnership with Sri Lanka, with the intent of making Sri Lanka a smart city and a commercial, naval, and aviation hub of Asia. In addition to analyzing opportunities for the city on a macro scale, the initiative will be seeking solutions to common issues in dense urban areas, like waste management, traffic, as well as focusing on resolving issues in slums and with environmental issues.

Open Data Initiatives

The Open Data movement is based on the idea that some data, mostly public data held by governments at the federal, state, and local levels, but also some scientific and academic data, should be openly available and free for anyone to use, analyze, and re-publish. (A related term, Open Government, is sometimes used interchangeably, but some Open Data advocates say this term should more strictly relate to the transparency of data specifically about government practices and policy—such as voting records and the funding sources for campaigns and elected officials.) In making this civic data available, governments allow for more innovative public-facing solutions to be developed.

On January 20, 2009, his first day in office, President Obama signed the Open Government Initiative, mandating that a great deal of government data become and remain available. This was followed in 2013 by Project Open Data, which provided resources and processes for storing civic data at the city, state, and federal levels to make these data sets publicly available. The administration maintains a website, data.gov, which serves as a repository for these downloadable data sets. At the time of this writing, there were over 5,100 data sets available in the local catalog for data relating to US cities—including crime statistics, business licenses, real-time traffic information, and many more. Anyone can download these data sets and cross-reference one against another, potentially discovering a pattern that might turn up a useful insight. And anyone who represents a government entity can upload a data set to the catalog, too.

By sharing these data sets in this way, new discoveries may emerge that lead to innovations to improve quality of life in cities and around the world.

Other data sources and insights

A variety of other sources of data are publicly available for download, as well. For example, bike share programs have risen in popularity in cities around the world. New York City's Citi Bike program alone had ten million rides in 2015. Citi Bike also makes system data available for mapping and analysis purposes.[85] The data they make accessible includes start and end times, ride duration, and start and end stations, all of which could spell out some behavioral patterns at a macro level. And for subscribers, they include birth year and gender, so it's possible to see demographic trends, as well. They include a unique identifier for each bike in the system, but there is no identifier for the system user, so the kinds of analysis that might see subscriber patterns over time isn't possible with this public data. But no doubt Citi Bike has that data and can analyze it themselves.

The Citi Bike system data as viewed in Microsoft Excel

Naturally, we might start to wonder about what this data suggests about connection to place and how the human data being tracked demonstrates it. It stands to reason that there are, for example, commuter uses of the service. On his blog, software developer Todd Schneider demonstrates this with some analysis of the freely available rider data.[86]

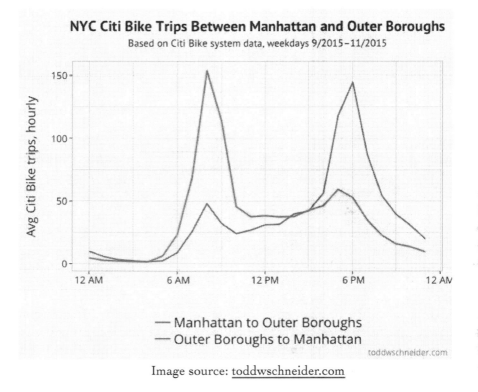

NYC Citi Bike Trips Between Manhattan and Outer Boroughs
Based on Citi Bike system data, weekdays 9/2015–11/2015

— Manhattan to Outer Boroughs
— Outer Boroughs to Manhattan

toddwschneider.com

Image source: toddwschneider.com

I find it interesting that the peaks of the two spikes don't line up perfectly. The gap there allows us to speculate about some scenarios that might make up the difference. Some of the people who ride from the outer boroughs to work in Manhattan in the morning (the red peak) may be meeting friends for drinks after work, or attending networking functions in the evening, and choosing to ride home later in the evening (note that the blue line is higher than the red past the peak), or take the subway home, or a cab. Maybe Brooklynites (and others) who work in Manhattan just work longer hours than Manhattanites who work in Brooklyn. That seems like a silly potential explanation, but it's kind of a provocative idea, and a puzzle we could begin to solve with more data. Once again, data can raise as many questions as it answers.

Balance and Flow

Every person will have a different threshold for adventure and excitement, but one of the promising ideas in designing experiences for humans with behavioral data insights is the chance to provide novel opportunities amidst the everyday.

For example, there's this great sense of serendipity about new places, and exploring the unknown. But there's also a great risk in going somewhere unfamiliar and taking the chance of not knowing how to get back.

This relates back to the part early on about GPS navigation and our innate sense of direction and observation of landmarks. (Recall that people had less ability to recall landmarks when they were using an "ego-centric" mapping experiences.) As it turns out, people may need to be able to explore to get their bearings and understand a place.

Perhaps one way to think about a "smart city" is simply as a city in which a visitor can get lost and not feel lost where there's enough infrastructure to guide them back.

At any rate, it's an interesting goal in almost any context: to design experiences so that a person can get lost without feeling lost.

Design experiences so that a person can get lost without feeling lost.

One lesson to take from cities is to design for "flow." In other words, to think not just about throughput and traffic maximization—not just about sales—but to remove obstacles that people might encounter as they go about their routines.

Most cities were designed around the car. But as cities have grown in density, cars are increasingly inefficient forms of transportation. Public transit like buses and trains is far more efficient, so in growing cities, there is a need for what is known as *transit-oriented design*. That's design that takes into account where subway stations and resources overlap; where bus routes are taken into consideration in the location scouting for a hospital; or where at least the transit authority is in discussions with the hospital about extending a bus route to the hospital. Good urban planning keeps these things in mind.

Part of applying this in integrated experience design is to think about how you accommodate multi-modality. For example, in cities throughout the United States, there are instances where, to merge onto a bridge, bicyclists have to cross car traffic at an intersection. Not only does that scenario pit bicyclists against motorists, but it also reveals an inherent bias for the cars. Websites that favor desktop browsers over phones and other mobile devices feel somewhat related to this paradigm (even if the desktops pose significantly less threat of harm to the phones). That extends, too, to brand interactions that don't attempt to interact with people in integrative physical and digital interactions.

The only way to scale a place or a system is by accommodating multiple modes of access in context-relevant ways. If your system doesn't adapt, it won't scale.

Another lesson from cities about access has to do with parking in a downtown area. Prohibitive parking costs may affect whether people who live outside of downtown spend time and money in the area. On the other hand, you could look at rising parking costs as an indicator that the downtown areas isn't as accessible by other modes as it could be. What are the implications, economically or otherwise, of optimizing your systems for infrequent use?

It's going to depend on your business and your brand: in a hotel geared at business travelers, it probably makes sense to design around frequent visitors to make the experience very familiar and comfortable for returning guests, but along the way also make things simple for those who are new to the brand. In an app relying on adoption by a critical mass of new and occasional users, on the other hand, the simplicity of the experience is key to ongoing success, but there still has to be something in it for the returning people.

In any case, what this gets at, fundamentally, is the need to think and design at scale—to consider what happens when something succeeds, and not let success be the downfall of a place or a system.

As most places and systems scale, it's imperative to keep people moving, which brings us right back to the metaphors of movement and stillness. (See the earlier section on "Movement Versus Stillness.") Part of our experience of a place is with our kinesthetic sense through its metaphors of movement or stillness, which means we can make meaning from motion, whether that motion is physical or imagined. Disconnected experiences have a sense of unease; integrated experiences don't always move fast, but they move forward deliberately.

***

One interesting facet of this, metaphorically, is that the best way to get meaningfully lost in a city you want to explore is on foot. Biking is fine and certainly gets you farther faster, but walking gives you more options and agility. And cars, buses, and subways are only so useful; they can get you from one part of town to the other, but to really take in the detail on a block-by-block level, you're better off on foot.

What's the analogy online? What does this tell us about experiencing online spaces and community?

There's a certain intentionality about it. You have to go into it with a mindset that you yourself are as much a part of the surroundings as everything you see.

In the old days, you could go online, hit a bookmark, do what you needed to do, and get out. That was one way of experiencing the internet. That was 1.0.

You could wade in and explore, immerse yourself, allow yourself to "surf" and float, then go where the links take you. That takes up an expansive amount of time. That was 2.0. (Or was it 1.5?)

Or you can be social and contribute. 3.0. (Or was that 2.0?)

Or you can experience the internet and everything it has spun off and empowered as an integrated part of your day-to-day life, being prompted with timely and relevant notifications by your devices, summoning a virtual assistant or search engine to answer questions as they arise, even having your surroundings adapt to you as you move through space. You move through space powered by data; you leave data in your wake; you *are* the digital self you create. Maybe this is what 4.0 is, or maybe it doesn't matter anymore what "version" it is. This isn't just about the internet anymore; this is our real life now. *That's* the experience we're heading into.

CHAPTER FOURTEEN

Epilogue: Where Do We Go From Here?

From smart fitting room mirrors to emailing a wrench to space, these are sweeping, big ideas, many of which fundamentally change our expectations of everyday encounters and interactions. This is not the realm of science fiction, although it sometimes feels like it. To use a metaphor of place to describe a state of being, this is where we are.

So if this is where we are, where do we go from here?

We embrace the integration, and we do so while creating meaningful experiences—the kind that we ourselves might want to have.

The Challenge: Follow the Integrated Human Experience Design Philosophy

The challenge is to execute these ideas while following the Integrated Human Experience Design philosophy:

- Make meaningful use of metaphor
- Blur the lines, with intention
- Recognize the humanity in the data

Furthermore, don't forget that:

Analytics are (often about) people. It's important to remind ourselves of the human beings represented by the data we collect and analyze.

Relevance is a form of respect, so show people what you offer that you think they'll want to see. But remember discretion is a form of respect, too. So gather the data you need, but don't be creepy.

***

The big takeaway is: it's all about the human experience. So we must be mindful when we create human experience to make it rich, with more nuance, more meaning, more connectedness.

I'll see you on the other side of the convergence.

Kate O'Neill has a rare expertise: she can recognize and articulate the potential for meaningful human experiences in everyday marketing strategy, and in doing so, can help companies make more money and add lasting value. She has a history of pioneering big ideas in the marketing industry: she was an early voice for advocating empathy combined with data to guide experience optimization, and brought a meaningfulness model to marketing strategy. Her career has likewise been a series of firsts: after building the first departmental website at the University of Illinois at Chicago, she was recruited to Toshiba in San Jose, California, and built their first intranet, shortly after which she held the first content management role at Netflix. Kate also founded digital strategy and analytics firm [meta]marketer, led cutting-edge online optimization work at Magazines.com, and held leadership positions in a variety of digital content and technology start-ups.

Now founder and CEO of KO Insights, Kate describes herself as a tech humanist and cultural strategist, and helps organizations develop their approach to data-rich experience design so that it is successful for the organization as well as for all of the people who interact with it.

Kate writes prolifically and contributes to a variety of outlets about a wide range of topics, primarily at the intersection of data, humanity, and meaningful experiences. She has been profiled in *CNN Money*, *TIME*, *Forbes*, *USA Today*, and other national media. In addition, Kate is a vocal and visible advocate for women in technology, entrepreneurship, and leadership — she was featured by Google in their global campaign for women in entrepreneurship. She speaks regularly at industry conferences and private events, providing keynotes, participating in panel discussions, and leading workshops.

More information about Kate, including ways to connect, can be found at: http://www.koinsights.com/about/about-kate-oneill/

[1] Peter F. Drucker, *Management, Revised Edition* (New York: Collins, 2008), 99.

[2] Peter F. Drucker, *The Five Most Important Questions You Will Ever Ask About Your Organization* (San Francisco: Jossey-Bass, 2008), xii.

[3] Chris Buettner, "Where It's At: An Interview with Two Place-Based Experience Designers," *Create.Adobe.com*, http://create.adobe.com/2016/6/3/this_must_be_the_place_an_interview_with_two_place_based_experience_designers.html.

[4] See Yi-Fu Tuan, *Space and Place: The Perspective of Experience* (Minneapolis: University of Minnesota Press, 1977).

[5] Kerry Bodine, "How Does Service Design Relate To CX And UX?" *Forrester* (Kerry Bodine's blog), October 4, 2013, http://blogs.forrester.com/kerry_bodine/13-10-04-how_does_service_design_relate_to_cx_and_ux.

[6] "Gartner Says By 2017, U.S. Customers' Mobile Engagement Behavior Will Drive Mobile Commerce Revenue to 50 Percent of U.S. Digital Commerce Revnue," *Gartner.com*, January 28, 2015, http://www.gartner.com/newsroom/id/2971917.

[7] "Experience," *Wikipedia*, last modified June, 2016, https://en.wikipedia.org/wiki/Experience.

[8] See B. Joseph Pine II and James H. Gilmore, *The Experience Economy: Updated Edition* (Boston: Harvard Business Review Press, 2011).

[9] David McCandless, "The beauty of data visualization," TED Talk, 17:56, July 2010, http://www.ted.com/talks/david_mccandless_the_beauty_of_data_visualization.

[10] Marcus Foth, "Why we should design smart cities for getting lost," *TheConversation.com*, April 7, 2016, https://theconversation.com/why-we-should-design-smart-cities-for-getting-lost-56492.

[11] Martin Lindstrom, *Brandwashed* (New York: Crown, 2012) 46–51.

[12] Tony Costa, "Brief: Disney Leads The Charge Across The Digital-Physical Divide," *Forrester.com*, April 24, 2014, https://www.forrester.com/report/Brief+Disney+Leads+The+Charge+Across+The+DigitalPhysical+Divide/-/E-RES115793.

[13] "Internet of Things to overtake mobile phones by 2018: Ericsson

Mobility Report," *Ericsson.com*, June 1, 2016, https://www.ericsson.com/news/2016987.

[14] Michael Chui, Markus Löffler, and Roger Roberts, "The Internet of Things," *McKinsey.com*, March 2010, http://www.mckinsey.com/industries/high-tech/our-insights/the-internet-of-things.

[15] Chante Owens, "Stranger hacks family's baby monitor and talks to child at night," The San Francisco Globe, August 4, 2016, http://sfglobe.com/2016/01/06/stranger-hacks-familys-baby-monitor-and-talks-to-child-at-night/.

[16] James Bamford, "The NSA Is Building the Country's Biggest Spy Center (Watch What You Say)," *Wired.com*, March 15, 2012, https://www.wired.com/2012/03/ff_nsadatacenter/all/1.

[17] Max Knoblauch, "Internet Users Send 204 Million Emails Per Minute," *Mashable.com*, April 23, 2014, http://mashable.com/2014/04/23/data-online-every-minute/#BNn9JfIDzSqx.

[18] See Surowiecki, James. *The Wisdom of Crowds*. (New York: Doubleday, 2004).

[19] "What is Placemaking?," Project for Public Spaces, http://www.pps.org/reference/what_is_placemaking/.

[20] Ibid.

[21] Jan Gehl, Lars Gemzøe, Sia Kirknæs, and Britt Sternhagen Søndergaard, *New City Life* (Copenhagen: Arkitektens Forlag [Danish Architectural Press], 2006).

[22] Paula Segal, quoted in Oscar Perry Abello, "Finding the Value of a Vacant Lot by Tapping Into Neighborhood Memory," *NextCity.org*, December 1, 2015, https://nextcity.org/daily/entry/new-york-vacant-lots-neighborhood-use-596-acres.

[23] Jennifer Valentino-Devries, Jeremy Singer-Vine, and Ashkan Soltani, "Websites Vary Prices, Deals Based on Users' Information," *WSJ.com*, December 24, 2012, http://www.wsj.com/articles/SB10001424127887323777204578189391813881534.

[24] Walt Hickey, "Be Suspicious Of Online Movie Ratings, Especially Fandango's," *FiveThirtyEight.com*, October 15, 2015, http://fivethirtyeight.com/features/fandango-movies-ratings/.

[25] Adam Withal, "Uber knows when your phone is running out of battery," *Independent*, May 22, 2016, http://www.independent.co.uk/life-style/gadgets-and-tech/news/uber-knows-when-your-phone-is-about-to-run-out-of-battery-a7042416.html.

[26] Mark Prigg, "Am I boring you? Google Glass app can read the emotions of everyone you talk to (and tell you how old they REALLY are)," *DailyMail.co.uk*, August 28, 2014, http://www.dailymail.co.uk/sciencetech/article-2737090/Am-I-boring-Google-glass-app-read-emotions-talk-tell-old-REALLY-are.html.

[27] Jay Bennett, "'Facewatch' Security Cams Give Store Owners a Taste of What It's Like to Be Big Brother," *PopularMechanics.com*, December 18, 2015, http://www.popularmechanics.com/technology/a18636/facewatch-facial-recognition-identify-criminals/.

[28] Lee Rainie and Maeve Duggan, "Privacy and Information Sharing," Pew Research Center, January 14, 2016, http://www.pewinternet.org/2016/01/14/privacy-and-information-sharing/.

[29] Ibid.

[30] David Chaum, "The Next Social Media We Want and Need!" *Backchannel*, January 19, 2016, https://backchannel.com/the-next-social-media-we-want-and-need-2d03a7e0551c#.3wrzcbb99.

[31] PSFK Labs, "Finding the Line Between Data Collection and Authenticity," *PSFK.com*, December 16, 2015, http://www.psfk.com/2015/12/mastercard-safety-and-security-data-collection-authenticity-online-protection-tim-hwang-interview.html.

[32] Ibid.

[33] George Lakoff, *Women, Fire, and Dangerous Things: What Categories Reveal About the Mind* (Chicago: University of Chicago Press, 1990).

[34] George Lakoff and Mark Johnson, *Metaphors We Live By* (Chicago: University of Chicago Press, 2003), 5.

[35] Josh Friedlander and Cara Duckworth, "Vinyl (Still) Rocks \m/!" *RIAA*, March 23, 2016, http://www.riaa.com/vinyl-still-rocks/.

[36] Diana Budds, "Rem Koolhaas: 'Architecture Has a Serious Problem Today,'" *Fast Company*, May 21, 2016, http://www.fastcodesign.com/3060135/innovation-by-design/rem-koolhaas-architecture-has-a-serious-problem-today.

[37] David Owen, "The Psychology of Space," *New Yorker*, January 21, 2013, http://www.newyorker.com/magazine/2013/01/21/the-psychology-of-space.

[38] Erin Kissane, "Content & Curation: An Epic Poem,"

[39] Christopher Thomas, "Maps: The Key Ingredient that Aggregates the Internet of Things (Industry Perspective)," *GovTech.com*, June 27, 2016, http://www.govtech.com/applications/Maps-Key-Ingredient-

Aggregates-Internet-of-Things-Industry-Perspective.html.

[40] Chris Milk, "How virtual reality can create the ultimate empathy machine," TED Talk, 10:16, March 2015, https://www.ted.com/talks/chris_milk_how_virtual_reality_can_create_the_ultimate_empathy_machine.

[41] Justin Jouvenal, "The new way police are surveilling you: Calculating your threat 'score'," *The Washington Post*, January 10, 2016, https://www.washingtonpost.com/local/public-safety/the-new-way-police-are-surveilling-you-calculating-your-threat-score/2016/01/10/e42bccac-8e15-11e5-baf4-bdf37355da0c_story.html.

[42] Byron Spice, "Questioning the Fairness of Targeting Ads Online," Carnegie Mellon University, July 7, 2015, http://www.cmu.edu/news/stories/archives/2015/july/online-ads-research.html.

[43] Eli Pariser, "Beware online 'filter bubbles,'" TED Talk, March 2011, 9:04, https://www.ted.com/talks/eli_pariser_beware_online_filter_bubbles?language=en.

[44] Maria Popova, "The Backfire Effect: The Psychology of Why We Have a Hard Time Changing Our Minds," *BrainPickings*, http://www.brainpickings.org/index.php/2014/05/13/backfire-effect-mcraney/.

[45] Michael Nielsen, "Is AlphaGo Really Such a Big Deal?" *QuantaMagazine.com*, March 29, 2016, https://www.quantamagazine.org/20160329-why-alphago-is-really-such-a-big-deal/.

[46] John Markoff, "A Learning Advance in Artificial Intelligence Rivals Human Abilities," *NYTimes.com*, December 10, 2015, http://www.nytimes.com/2015/12/11/science/an-advance-in-artificial-intelligence-rivals-human-vision-abilities.html.

[47] "Machine-Learning Algorithm Identifies Tweets Sent Under the Influence of Alcohol," *MIT Technology Review*, March 16, 2016, https://www.technologyreview.com/s/601051/machine-learning-algorithm-identifies-tweets-sent-under-the-influence-of-alcohol/.

[48] Alex Kantrowitz, "Google Is Feeding Romance Novels To Its Artificial Intelligence Engine To Make Its Products More Conversational," *BuzzFeed News*, May 4, 2016, https://www.buzzfeed.com/alexkantrowitz/googles-artificial-intelligence-engine-reads-romance-novels.

[49] Rick Robinson, "3 human qualities digital technology can't replace in the future economy: experience, values and judgement,"

The Urban Technologist.com, April 12, 2015, http://
theurbantechnologist.com/2015/04/12/3-human-qualities-digital-
technology-cant-replace-in-the-future-economy-experience-values-and-
judgement/.

[50] Linda Poon, "Finally, an App That Gives You Directions Like a
Human Would," *Citylab*, December 16, 2015, http://www.citylab.com/
navigator/2015/12/finally-an-app-that-gives-you-directions-like-a-
human-would/420792/.

[51] Sarah Guo, "The Conversational Economy Part 1: What's Causing
the Bot Craze?" *VentureBeat*, June 13, 2016, http://venturebeat.com/
2016/06/13/the-conversational-economy-part-1-whats-causing-the-bot-
craze/.

[52] Venkatakrishnan Balasubramanian, "Five Dimensions to
Conceptualize Your Idea to Make it a Successful Innovation,"
InnovationMangagement.se, http://www.innovationmanagement.se/
2012/01/23/how-to-build-a-framework-to-conceptualize-your-ideas-
into-successful-innovations/.

[53] Karl Gustafson, "Why Measurement Alone Will Not Lead to Better
Marketing," *AdvertisingAge*, February 23, 2010, http://adage.com/article/
cmo-strategy/measurement-lead-marketing/142261/.

[54] "Space Station 3-D Printer Builds Ratchet Wrench To Complete
First Phase Of Operations," *Nasa.gov*, December 22, 2014, http://
www.nasa.gov/mission_pages/station/research/news/
3Dratchet_wrench.

[55] "Don't Go There. Live There," YouTube video, 1:00, posted by
Airbnb, April 19, 2016, https://www.youtube.com/watch?
v=1AtjOKph7-k.

[56] Donal Power, "GE and Hitachi see IIoT unlocking the next
industrial revolution," *readwrite.com*, July 1, 2016, http://readwrite.com/
2016/07/01/ge-hitachi-see-iiot-unlocking-next-industrial-revolution-il4/.

[57] Abi Mandelbaum, "Can Beacons Inspire Guests to Digitally Interact
with Hotels?" *Lodgingmagazine.com*, March 3, 2015, http://
lodgingmagazine.com/can-beacons-inspire-guests-to-digitally-interact-
with-hotels/.

[58] Jim Shea, "True Detective: First Insight Finds What Consumers
Really Want from Retailers," *FirstInsight*, August 12, 2015, http://
www.firstinsight.com/press-releases/true-detective-first-insight-finds-
what-consumers-really-want-from-retailers.

[59] Ibid.

[60] Neha Malik, "How Hotels can use Beacons to Enhance Guest Experiences," *beaconstac.com*, July 8, 2014, http://blog.beaconstac.com/2014/07/how-hotels-can-use-beacons-to-enhance-guest-experiences/.

[61] In his 1957 book, *Interpreting Our Heritage*, Freeman Tilden defined six principles of interpretation:

1. Any interpretation that does not somehow relate what is being displayed or described to something within the personality or experience of the visitor will be sterile.

2. Information, as such, is not Interpretation. Interpretation is revelation based upon information. But they are entirely different things. However all interpretation includes information.

3. Interpretation is an art, which combines many arts, whether the materials presented are scientific, historical or architectural. Any art is in some degree teachable.

4. The chief aim of Interpretation is not instruction, but provocation.

5. Interpretation should aim to present a whole rather than a part, and must address itself to the whole man rather than any phase.

6. Interpretation addressed to children (say up to the age of twelve) should not be a dilution of the presentation to adults, but should follow a fundamentally different approach. To be at its best it will require a separate program.

https://en.wikipedia.org/wiki/Heritage_interpretation

[62] "Deaths From Unintentional Injury Among Adults Aged 65 and Over: United States, 2000–2013," *Centers for Disease Control and Prevention*, May 2015,

http://www.cdc.gov/nchs/data/databriefs/db199.htm.

[63] Eric Boodman, "To keep seniors living independently, sensors track their home habits," *STAT*, December 31, 2015, https://www.statnews.com/2015/12/31/remote-monitoring-elderly/.

[64] Matt Phillips, "No one cooks anymore," *Quartz.com*, June 14, 2016, http://qz.com/706550/no-one-cooks-anymore/.

[65] Melanie Evans, "Hospitals face closures as 'a new day in healthcare' dawns," Modern Healthcare, February 21, 2015, http://www.modernhealthcare.com/article/20150221/MAGAZINE/302219988.

[66] "Fact Sheet: Two-Midnight Rule," Centers for Medicare & Medicaid

Services, July 01, 2015, https://www.cms.gov/Newsroom/MediaReleaseDatabase/Fact-sheets/2015-Fact-sheets-items/2015-07-01-2.html.

[67] "E-health in practice," World Health Organization, March 10, 2016, http://www.euro.who.int/en/data-and-evidence/news/news/2016/01/e-health-in-practice.

[68] "Free super fast Wi-Fi. And that's just the beginning," *LinkNYC.com*, https://www.link.nyc/?_ga=1.255514632.1499394577.1467406494.

[69] Lauren Walker, "The Risks of Connecting to New York's New, Free Wi-Fi," *Newsweek.com*, November 19, 2014, http://www.newsweek.com/risks-connecting-new-yorks-new-free-wi-fi-285377.

[70] James Manyika, Michael Chui, Peter Bisson, Jonathan Woetzel, Richard Dobbs, Jacques Bughin, and Dan Aharon, "Unlocking the potential of the Internet of Things," *McKinsey.com*, June 2015, http://www.mckinsey.com/business-functions/business-technology/our-insights/the-internet-of-things-the-value-of-digitizing-the-physical-world.

[71] "Retail Spend on 'Internet of Things' to Reach $2.5BN by 2020," *Juniper Research*, September 1, 2015, http://www.juniperresearch.com/press/press-releases/retail-spend-on-iot-to-reach-2-5bn-by-2020.

[72] "Top retail holiday trends: Holiday shopping survey results 2015," *AccentureConsulting*, https://www.accenture.com/insight-top-retail-holiday-trends-holiday-shopping-survey-results-2015.

[73] David Kaplan, "Target Rolls Out Beacons At 50 Stores—With Bigger Plans To Come," *GeoMarketing*, August 5, 2015, http://www.geomarketing.com/target-rolls-out-beacons-at-50-stores-with-bigger-plans-to-come.

[74] "The IKEA Pop-up is open. Come on in!" *IKEA.com*, http://www.ikea.com/ms/en_CA/great_offers/popup.html.

[75] Amar Toor, "Amazon plans to open more retail stores," *The Verge*, May 18, 2016, http://www.theverge.com/2016/5/18/11699544/amazon-new-retail-locations-prime-bezos.

[76] Lauren Johnson, "Here Are 4 Tips From a Startup That's About to Go Global," *Adweek*, November 6, 2015, http://www.adweek.com/news/technology/here-are-4-tips-startup-thats-about-go-global-168001.

[77] https://casper.com/naptour

[78] Lauryn Chamberlain, "Online to Offline: How Opening Retail Stores Helped Rent The Runway Spike Site Traffic," *GeoMarketing*, February 29, 2016, http://www.geomarketing.com/online-to-offline-

how-opening-retail-stores-helped-rent-the-runway-spike-site-traffic

[79] "Smart fitting rooms: AdvanFitting," *Keonn*, http://keonn.com/systems/view-all-3/smart-fitting-rooms.html.

[80] Simon Davies, "The Smart Fitting Room Is the Future of Retail," *Tech.co*, December 17, 2015, http://tech.co/smart-fitting-room-future-retail-2015-12.

[81] "Food Trucks Primarily Replace a Quick Service Restaurant Visit, Says NPD," *NPD.com*, August 19, 2013, https://www.npd.com/wps/portal/npd/us/news/press-releases/food-trucks-primarily-replace-a-quick-service-restaurant-visit-says-npd/.

[82] Promothesh Chatterjee and Randall L. Rose, "Do Payment Mechanisms Change the Way Consumers Perceive Products?" *Journal of Consumer Research* 38.6 (2012), http://jcr.oxfordjournals.org/content/38/6/1129.abstract.

[83] Elena Wang, "The Origins of Pop-Up Shops," *Zady.com*, https://zady.com/features/the-origins-of-pop-up-shops.

[84] "Placemaking Meets Preservation," *Project for Public Spaces*, July 15, 2010, http://www.pps.org/blog/placemaking-meets-preservation/.

[85] "System Data," *CitiBikeNYC.com*, 2016, https://www.citibikenyc.com/system-data.

[86] Todd W. Schneider, "A Tale of Twenty-Two Million Citi Bike Rides: Analyzing the NYC Bike Share System," January 13, 2016, http://toddwschneider.com/posts/a-tale-of-twenty-two-million-citi-bikes-analyzing-the-nyc-bike-share-system/

Made in the USA
Lexington, KY
08 September 2016